EGYPT

The Thornton Cox Guide

EGYPT

A concise guide for independent travellers

PENELOPE TURING

THORNTON
COX

Distribution:
Distributed in Great Britain and the Commonwealth by
Roger Lascelles, 47 York Road, Brentford, Middlesex TW8 0QP
Telephone: (081) 847 0935

ISBN 0 902726 48 X

Distributed in the United States and Canada by
Hippocrene Books Inc., 171 Madison Avenue, New York NY 10016

US ISBN 0 87052 143 8

Published 1992 by Thornton Cox (1986) Ltd,
4 Baches Street, London N1 6UB

Published in the United States and Canada by
Hippocrene Books Inc., 171 Madison Avenue, New York NY 10016

First published by Geographia Ltd 1982.
Second edition, fully revised, September 1988.
This revised edition, January 1992

Drawings by GUY MAGNUS
Maps by Tom Stalker-Miller, MSIA
Series editor: Kit Harding
Cover: Pyramids at Giza, by Bernard Régent, Hutchison Library
Photographs not otherwise credited by courtesy of Egyptian Tourist Authority

Great care has been taken throughout this book to be accurate,
but the publishers cannot accept responsibility for any errors
which appear or for their consequences. Prices quoted were correct
at the time of publication.

Printed in Great Britain by The Guernsey Press Company Limited,
Guernsey, Channel Islands. Set in 8½ on 9½ Univers

Thornton Cox Guides:

Titles in print in this series include:

Mediterranean France	**Kenya & Northern Tanzania**	**Portugal**
Greece	**Southern Africa**	
Ireland	**Southern Spain**	

Feluccas on the Nile

Contents

Author's Acknowledgements

The author gratefully acknowledges the facilities and assistance provided by the Egyptian Tourist Authority and their staff, and by EgyptAir during research work in Egypt for this book.

Foreword

If the visitor flies in to Cairo Airport by day, the contrasts which make Egypt one of the most fascinating countries in the world are symbolised in the colours of the land. Ridges of the desert hills appear no larger than the hard rippled sand encountered on the western beaches of childhood. As the plane descends they grow into great contours, clean, anonymous, bright golden in the sunshine until they meet the sharp green ribbon of cultivation.

Nearly 2,500 years ago, the Greek writer Herodotus described Egypt as the gift of the Nile. Where its waters by natural flooding or artificial irrigation have spread over the desert there is richly fertile land, clearly marked along the Nile Valley and the Delta or by isolated oases where the desert is blessed with springs. Water is vital for life: yet although the Nile floods were sacred to the ancient Egyptians it was the sun that they worshipped. To them, the sun was more powerful than the waters.

Today this pattern still holds good. It is by irrigation and water power that the country is developing, and must develop to support a rapidly growing population. But it is the sun and the dry desert atmosphere that has protected and preserved the archaeological treasures of the past. In northern Europe damp and frost would have split and eroded these temples and statues long before the Christian era. Here the dryness and the sheltering sands have helped them to survive. Nonetheless changed circumstances are bringing new problems. The huge expanse of water which is Nasser Lake has altered the immemorial pattern and traps the fertile Nile silt which was formerly carried downstream to nourish irrigated fields. Atmospheric pollution too is at work, and even the breathing of many tourists in the restricted spaces of tombs and temples is causing more damage in a generation than the wind and sun have inflicted in many centuries.

Tourism is traditionally an important industry for Egypt. From the time of Alexander the Great (332 BC), Greeks and Romans came as conquerors and stayed to wonder at the heritage of Egypt's art and culture. Since then, much has been added to the land of the pharaohs. St Mark himself is believed to have brought Christianity to Egypt — the country to which the Holy Family fled for safety from Herod — and the Coptic Church was established. Islam came in the 7th century with the Arab invasion which swept westwards through North Africa. Overall it is a many-cultured, many-splendoured land. The purpose of this book is to provide an outline of what it is and has to offer, and a few guidelines on how to approach it.

Foreword

Egypt is also an exciting, developing state, full of young people, which many visitors may fail to experience if they concentrate only on pharaonic marvels and tourist shops and souks.

Egyptians are passionately keen on education and many of the most highly qualified work in the wealthier Arab states to support their families at home. But crises abroad can take away the jobs. For these and other reasons there are still areas of great need and of poverty, despite so much being done. Both progress and problems, however, make Egypt an absorbingly interesting country.

Tourism is, of course, still one of the country's vital industries and it has been extensively and well developed. During the past ten years there has been amazing progress and many improvements have been made, not least to the road system. The main highways, often dual carriageway, are well surfaced, signposting is good and clear and on all major routes is in English and Arabic. Where once traffic jams were endemic and airports chaotic, this is no longer so. The centre of Cairo, and perhaps even more of Alexandria, can suffer appalling traffic jams at rush hours — particularly lunchtime — but the Cairo flyovers and the ring road behind Alexandria have helped enormously. Cairo airport now works smoothly and efficiently, as do the smaller airports at Luxor, Aswan and Mersa Matruh. There is also a marked improvement in cleanliness. Transportation is often better than you expect: there are good train services (and some dirty ones), good long distance coaches, domestic air services, local buses and trams, and Cairo now has an underground railway. All are cheap by European standards, and hotel rates are moderate.

For the inexperienced, and this is not a derogatory term but includes many who travel extensively but do not want to be bothered with the details of reservations, transportation and so on, by far the best plan is to take a package holiday. Many are available, in a number of different price categories. Some are very expensive and these include some — but not all — of the Nile cruises, which undoubtedly form the most restful and delightful way of exploring the treasures of the Nile Valley from Luxor up to Aswan. Other packages are cheaper, offering the best value for money because they include the air fare from Britain or America or other countries.

With an inclusive holiday of this kind everything is arranged. If hitches occur, and they do from time to time in most tourist countries of the world, there is usually someone at hand who must sort the problem out for you. This is a considerable advantage if you do not know the country and its people, since Egypt can be very bewildering and also very irritating.

Egyptians are genuinely friendly and usually helpful, but they are inclined to say what they think will please you rather than what may be the unpalatable truth. Also, although English is widely spoken you will find the young are not so fluent as their elders who learned it when the British influence was strong. So, if you want an easy holiday, book an inclusive package. On the other hand, there are many people who prefer to be entirely independent, and it is true that one experiences much more of the atmosphere of the country and has a far better chance of getting to know the people if one is not in a group. The independent traveller may be of any age or income, from the very wealthy to the student.

For those who want to go it alone Egypt is a kindly, interesting country. A lot of patience is needed. There are times when you have to be firm, but usually a smiling patience and tenacity will achieve most of what you want.

The traveller's best passports here as in other Arab states are courtesy and understanding: a readiness to respect the traditions of the country and to give and receive friendship. Do not be afraid. The traffic of Cairo is dangerous but the people are not. You will be assailed by a few real beggars and some children seeking baksheesh, but you are less likely to be mugged in Cairo than in London.

Remember that a lot of bare flesh is not acceptable to Islamic convention for either men or women. Scanty beach wear should be worn only on private hotel beaches. Shorts are not worn by locals and, as one young British resident remarked to me, the wearer is considered fair game for exorbitant charges!

Throughout the country the visitor rarely meets with anything but interest and a willingness to please. The worst problems — and they are many — stem from bureaucratic administration. This often tries the western patience, but one cannot understand Egypt without attempting to grasp the reasons for its idiosyncracies. It is government policy to try to find work for as many as possible of its rapidly growing population. The result is that you will sometimes find six men doing one man's job, which does not make for speed or efficiency.

For those who are really interested in knowing the country and its people a remarkable organisation exists called the Tourist Friends' Association, (see General Information). For those content with the historical panorama, Egypt will create its own unique and almost unreal aura.

Throughout the book, prices quoted are given as examples only and are therefore liable to change.

General Information

How to get there

By Air

Almost all visitors travelling from Great Britain, Europe, America or Japan to Egypt will make the journey by air, arriving at the international airport at Heliopolis, 23 kilometres (15 miles) north east of Cairo. EgyptAir, the national airline, runs a daily non-stop service between London (Heathrow) and Cairo, flights taking four and three-quarter hours. They also have a service to New York three times a week and twice a week to Tokyo, as well as services to about 50 other cities world wide. Alcohol is not served on EgyptAir flights. A number of the London-Cairo flights are by the new A-300 600 Airbus which provides extra comfort and enables you to watch the progress of your aircraft across a map of the route on the television screens.

British Airways also has non-stop flights between London (Gatwick) and Cairo five times a week. TWA flies New York-Cairo three times weekly (one stop).

EgyptAir office addresses are:
UK: 29 Piccadilly, London, W1; tel: 071 734 2864.
USA: 630 Fifth Avenue, New York, NY 10011; tel: 212 247 4880.
Japan: Palace Building, 1-1-1 Marunouchi (Chiyoda-Ku), Tokyo; tel: 211 452(03).

Air fares change so rapidly now that it is pointless to quote them here, but a wide range of different fares is available. Any reputable travel agent can supply current information on flights and fares.

Cairo Airport is spacious with a well marked meeting-point where tour operators meet clients on arrival. There are banks and refreshment buffets; baggage reclaim and Customs are quite efficient. Check-in for EgyptAir international departures tends to be slow. There is a good duty-free shop selling alcohol as well as other duty-free goods.

There are regular buses from the Airport to central Cairo, but it is better to take a 'limousine' which have fixed charges (about LE 22 to the city centre). Taxis are also available but you will have to bargain before starting (LE 10 is a fair price for the same journey). There are ranks for both limousines and taxis at the Airport.

By Sea

Some local Mediterranean cruises call at Alexandria, Port Said or Suez, enabling passengers to make a visit to Cairo and sometimes to Luxor before rejoining the ship after it has passed through the Suez Canal, but sea transport is no longer a regular route for holidaymakers and travellers visiting Egypt.

Ferries operated by Adriatica (London bookings through Sealink, tel. 071 828 1940) sail from Venice to Alexandria via Dubrovnik, Piraeus and Heraklion every 10 days, except mid January-mid March.

Travel within the country

Air

EgyptAir has frequent daily services from Cairo Airport to Abu Simbel, Alexandria, Aswan, Hurghada, Luxor; three times weekly to Mersa Matruh (summer only); twice weekly to New Valley: there are also services between Abu Simbel and Aswan, Aswan and Luxor, Luxor and New Valley. Air Sinai operates services Cairo-Hurghada (twice weekly), Cairo-St Catherine (twice weekly), Cairo-Sharm el Sheikh (five times weekly), El Arish (twice weekly), El Tor (twice weekly).

Domestic services in Egypt are usually efficient, clean, and provide light refreshment. Sometimes there are over-booking problems, or delays. Fares are reasonable. Book in advance: EgyptAir, 6 Adly Street, Cairo; tel. 391 1256. Air Sinai office is at the Nile Hilton Hotel.

Red Sea boat crossing

It is possible to cross the Red Sea by boat from Hurghada to Sharm el Sheikh, a six-hour voyage, on Sundays, Tuesdays, and Thursdays; from Sharm to Hurghada on Mondays, Wednesdays and Saturdays. Charge in 1990 LE 50 each way. Book locally or with Spring Tours, 3 El Sayed El Bakri, Zamalek, Cairo; tel. 5972/5.

Rail

There are rail services Cairo-Luxor-Aswan with good 'new' air-conditioned sleeping cars on the night service run by Wagons-Lits. There are also much cheaper old sleeping cars.

There are rail services Cairo-Ismailia-Port Said; Cairo-Suez; Cairo-Alexandria-Mersa Matruh. First class is generally good and air conditioned; second class sometimes air conditioned; third class primitive.

General Information

Coach and bus services

A good network of long distance coaches, many air conditioned, links Cairo with Alexandria, the Canal cities — Port Said, Ismailia and Suez, and the Nile towns of Upper Egypt. They also go to Hurghada and between Hurghada and Luxor. There are services to Sinai — Cairo to Sharm el Sheikh, Cairo to St Catherine's — and right across to Taba, which is the Egyptian frontier crossing to Eilat in Israel on the Gulf of Aqaba. Another bus service goes from Cairo across Sinai to Nuweiba, where a three-hour ferry voyage takes you to Aqaba, then another bus to Jordan's capital Amman.

Yet another service goes across northern Sinai to El Arish, another into Israel to Tel Aviv. These are all long and rather exhausting journeys — about 12 hours from Cairo to Aqaba — but fares are very modest.

Principal bus stations in Cairo are Tahrir Square; Ramsses main Railway Station; Ramsses Street, Abbassia; and (on the west bank of the Nile) Giza Square. Check with tourist office or travel agent for your departure point and advance booking office for the service you require.

Local buses are an experience well worth sampling in the country districts, and very cheap. In Cairo they tend to be overcrowded and it is difficult for the non-Arabic speaker to find the right one, and to know where to get off.

Metro

Cairo now has the first line of its underground railway. Important stations are Mubarak (Ramsses Square central Railway Station) and Sadat (Tahrir Square); there is another, Mar Girges, for Old Cairo. The line continues beyond this to Helwan. Short journey fare 35 piastres; Sadat-Helwah 50 piastres.

Taxis

Taxis are checkered black and white. Few drivers switch on their meters (official rates are very low) and it is necessary to negotiate before starting. LE 2 or LE 3 is a fair payment in the city centre, but you may have to pay more if there are few taxis about. In any case they are cheap because of the rate of exchange (see 'Currency'). But Egyptian taxis are always a problem for the visitor. Do not be surprised if the driver gives a lift to a friend or stranger in the front seat without asking your permission. Limousines ply from the hotels at a high fixed rate.

Hire cars

Self-drive for the courageous (own insurance and international driving licence required) and chauffeur-driven cars are available: Avis, Hertz and Budget Rental. Bookings through airlines or hotels.

All over the country there are now good, clear road signs in English and Arabic, white on blue.

Banks and currency

Banks open from 0830 to 1400 from Sunday to Thursday. Banking offices in major hotels are open at other times.

The Egyptian Pound (LE) = 100 Piastres. Notes are of 10, 25 and 50 piastres and LE 1, 5, 10 and 20. Coins are of 5, 10 and 20 piastres.

The UK Exchange Rate is £1 = LE 5.20 approximately, but this should be checked.

Credit cards: Access/Mastercard, American Express, Diners Club and Visa are accepted.

Currency restrictions: tourists can enter and leave Egypt with a maximum of LE 20. There are no restrictions on the import of foreign currency provided it is declared on an official customs form. Export of foreign currency is limited to the amount stated as the balance on the declaration form, which must not exceed the amount imported. **Keep all bank receipts** when you change travellers' cheques or foreign currency into LE as you will need these if you want to reconvert from LE at the end of your stay. This is a lengthy process, so do not exchange more than you need. You are expected to show that you have spent the equivalent of US$30 per day of your stay in Egypt if you seek to reconvert.

Churches and monasteries

Cairo
The most famous old Coptic churches in the capital are in the area on the east bank of the Nile called Old Cairo: St Sergius, El Mouallaqa and St Barbara, and visitors are welcomed at their services which — as in the Eastern Orthodox churches — are very long. It is necessary to enquire locally about the times of services. St Mark's Coptic Cathedral is at Abbassia, in north-east Cairo. There are many other Coptic churches throughout the capital, some built very recently.

The monasteries in Wadi Natrun can be visited without prior permission, but are closed to visitors at some seasons, such as Lent (Eastern dating). For information telephone the Coptic Cathedral, Ramesses St Abbassia, Cairo 282-5376. Permission to visit is required for the monasteries of St Paul and St Anthony near Ein Sukhna (about 60 km from Suez); for this ring the same number. NOTE that St Catherine's Monastery in Sinai is Greek Orthodox, not Coptic. Details in the Sinai chapter.

General Information

The new Episcopal (Anglican) All Saints Cathedral is behind the Marriott Hotel in Zamalek. There are Sunday services at 0800, 1030 and 1915 in English and Arabic.

St Joseph's Roman Catholic Church is at Ahmed Sabri St., Zamalek. Sunday Masses are at 0830 (Arabic), 1100 (French), 1800 (English), 1900 (French).

A German Evangelical Church is at 32 El Galaa Street, where the Sunday service is at 0930.

Alexandria

St Mark's Episcopal (Anglican) Church is in Tahrir Square. Sunday Holy Communion is at 1030.

St Catherine's Roman Catholic Cathedral, in St Catherine's Square, holds Sunday Masses at 0830 (English), 1000 (Arabic), 1200 (Italian), 1800 (French).

Climate

Egypt has a warm dry climate and is very hot in high summer. From October to May it is ideal for sightseeing, though it can be quite cold at night in winter: indeed the desert is almost always cold at night. Most modern hotels and many trains, cars and buses are air-conditioned which makes it more comfortable in summer, but those who dislike intense heat should avoid Upper Egypt from June to September. Summer is, however, the high season for Alexandria and the Mediterranean coast.

Spring is a very popular time, but it is fair to say that the khamseen wind may blow continuously for eight days any time between mid-February and early April, and this brings dust and sand storms in Upper Egypt, dust storms and sometimes rain in Cairo and high seas at Alexandria.

Average temperature in centigrade

		Cairo	Luxor	Aswan	Alexandria
Jan	min	8.6	5.4	9.4	9.3
	max	19.1	22.9	24.2	18.3
Apr	min	13.9	15.7	15.2	13.5
	max	28.2	34.8	35.6	23.6
Jul	min	21.5	23.6	26.1	22.7
	max	35.4	40.8	41.9	29.6
Oct	min	17,8	17.7	21.7	17.8
	max	29.9	35.1	37.5	27.7

Customs and Immigration

The following goods may be imported into Egypt free of duty: 200

cigarettes or 25 cigars or 200 grams of tobacco; one litre of spirits; one litre of perfume or toilet water; gifts up to the value of LE 500. All cash, travellers cheques, credit cards and gold over LE 500 must be declared on arrival. Prohibited items include drugs and firearms.

Entry formalities

A valid passport is required by all visitors. The passport should be valid for at least six months beyond the period of intended stay in Egypt. A British Visitors Passport is not acceptable.

A visa is also required by all visitors. There are two types of visa, tourist and business (both have single and multiple entry types). Tourist visas cost £15.00 for one journey; £18.00 for three journeys. Business visas cost £43.00 for one journey, and £68.00 for three journeys, provided a business letter is forwarded. Payment of fees are by cash or postal orders only. Cheques will not be accepted. Visa fees are per passport, not per person. Visas are valid for three months from date of issue or six months for multiple entry, and one month from date of arrival; they cannot be post-dated. Tourist Visas can also be obtained on arrival at Cairo Airport.

Applications should be made to:

UK: Egyptian Consulate, 19 Kensington Palace Gardens Mews, London W8; tel. 071 229 8818/9. Open 1000-1400 Monday to Friday.

USA: Egyptian Embassy, 2310 Decatur Palace NW, Washington DC 2008; tel. 202 234 3903.

Japan: Egyptian Embassy, 4-5 1 Chome Aobadai Megure-ku, Tokyo; tel. Tokyo 463 4504.

Application requirements are: one photograph; valid passport; application form. Allow 7-10 working days for issue of the visa.

Registration in Egypt

All visitors must be registered with the police within a week of arrival in the country. This registration is normally done by the hotel, or personal host where the visitor stays, not by the tourist (unless specifically asked to do so). Remember to ask for the return of your passport before departure for the next hotel!

If you are asked to make your own registration in Cairo (e.g. if you are staying with a family) the office is a very large building called Mugamma in Tahrir Square. Go to the 'box office' marked for the district in which you are staying.

South Sinai concession

Foreigners coming to Egypt through points of entry in South Sinai, to visit the area of Aqaba coast and St Catherine's, are allowed to enter without an entry visa to visit this area alone, for one week maximum. These points of entry are: the Taba land entry; St Catherine Airport; Ras Nosrany (Sharm El Sheikh) Airport, Sharm El Sheikh Seaport; Qaboos 'Nuweiba' temporary port. Such visitors are exempted from currency exchange regulations and from registering with the police, but they are not permitted to proceed to other parts of Egypt.

Diplomatic Representation

Among the 66 countries which have embassies in Cairo readers may require the following addresses:

UK: Embassy of Great Britain, Ahmed Ragheb Street, Garden City, Cairo; tel. 354 0850/9.

USA: United States Embassy, Lazougi St., Garden City, Cairo; tel. 355 7371.

Japan: Japanese Embassy, 3rd Floor, Cairo Centre, Building 2, Abdel Keder, Hamza St, Garden City, Cairo; tel. 355 3962.

Dress

In high summer the lightest cotton wear is cooler and more comfortable than man-made fabrics. During spring and autumn take lightweight suits and slacks for men, similar weight slacks and long sleeved blouses or thin sweaters for women. Always take one thin outfit. From December to March, light woollens may be needed. At all seasons it is advisable to take a coat, preferably one that can be packed in the suitcase, possibly for one's entire time in Egypt. A wrap for the evenings for women and a jacket or sweater for men is essential. Women will probably find one long dress useful if any formal occasion occurs, though you can buy a colourful galebeah locally which looks attractive and is cool and comfortable. The better hotels prefer men to wear a collar and tie in the restaurant, but it is not a rule.

Remember that Egypt is still a conservative country. To expose a lot of bare flesh except on the beach is not in good taste, so dresses or blouses and shirts with sleeves are a good choice. They will also protect you from excessive sunburn when standing about in the blazing heat at archaeological sites. The most important item of clothing is a pair of flat-heeled, strong, comfortable shoes. Sandals are good in the towns and on board ship, but for archaeological sites and the desert, covered shoes are essential. Most people will need sunglasses. A sun hat is also useful, especially in the summer:

swimming things too, because many hotels have a pool even if you are not by the sea.

Food and Drink

Egypt is not a particularly exciting country from the gastronomic point of view, especially in the hotels where most visitors stay. The best hotels will have an international cuisine, the lesser ones will either give you rather poorly prepared European dishes or — preferably — Egyptian food. Typical dishes include: *foul madhammas,* a national dish of fava beans cooked with spices and tomato, sometimes served with a fried egg on top; *shish kebab* is made of pieces of lamb specially spiced and marinaded before grilling; *shorbat adas* is a deliciously spiced lentil soup; pigeons, grilled or broiled on an open spit are another national dish and are very good. Fish is almost always a good choice: popular dishes include sea bass from the Mediterranean, tilapia from the Nile, or huge succulent prawns from the Red Sea.

Several quite pleasant wines come from the Alexandria region and though not cheap in restaurants they are certainly not expensive. The best known is the red *Omar Khayyam,* but there are also some good whites such as *Ptolemies. Ruby Egypt* is a rosé. Local beer is light and quite good. The majority of Egyptians, being Moslems, do not drink alcohol, so soft drinks are always available. But the visitor will rarely have difficulty in getting wine, beer or spirits when he wants them. *Karkade* is a soft drink made from hibiscus flowers, said to be good for high blood pressure.

Health

No vaccinations are officially required on entering Egypt, although if you are coming from a country which is recognised as an infected area for cholera or yellow fever, a certificate of innoculation is necessary. In any case, immunisation against the following diseases is recommended by the medical authorities in Britain for travellers visiting Egypt: cholera, infectious hepatitis (hepatitis A), poliomyelitis, tetanus and typhoid. Recommendations about malaria prophylaxis are not given when the country is officially 'malaria free'. However this situation is liable to change so it is always advisable to take anti-malaria tablets. 'Paludrine' is taken daily (2 tablets), 'Chloroquine' once a week (2 tablets); in each case start the course one week before arriving in Egypt, continue throughout the visit and for four weeks thereafter.

All necessary vaccinations and medical travel advice can be had from various centres such as the International Medical Centre, 21, Upper Wimpole St., London, W1M 7TA; tel. 071-486-3063. Alternatively the vaccinations can be given by your own doctor.

General Information

Many visitors suffer from the proverbial 'gyppy tummy' — diarrhoea and/or sickness. Usually, this develops about four days after arrival, is not serious and lasts only 24 to 48 hours. 'Imodium' (obtainable without prescription from chemists in UK) is generally an effective treatment. In Egypt (where European proprietory brands are not always easy to obtain because of high cost) 'Entocid' is an Egyptian product widely used and recommended, and readily obtainable. Consult a doctor if the trouble persists or if you are really ill. Hotels (some have a resident doctor) or tourist offices or travel agents will help you call a doctor. It is wise to specify an English-speaking one (or other language required). Fee for a visit can vary from LE 30 to LE 80. There are good private hospitals such as the Anglo-American Hospital (below Cairo Tower in Zamalek, Gezira Island) tel. 340-6163, but they are expensive. It is therefore important to take out a travellers' health insurance policy when booking your holiday, unless you have permanent overseas cover such as an American Express 'Centurion Assistance' policy. In general, it is advisable to avoid eating unwashed fruit and to drink only the bottled water. A good insect repellent is vital to all visitors as flies and mosquitoes are a menace throughout the country.

Hotels

Hotels in Egypt are graded five, four, three, two and one star. Room rates in the first three categories are quoted in US dollars, but can be paid for in Egyptian pounds, sterling or other hard currency (though some hotels seem reluctant to accept anything except US$ or LE). The Egyptian pound was devalued in July 1987. Local residents (who are suffering painful inflation) pay their dollar quotations at the exchange rate before devaluation — US$ 1 = LE 1.35. This can mean that an Egyptian may pay less than a visitor for an identical room, because visitors pay at the current exchange rate, in summer 1991 US$ = LE 3.30. Thus five-star hotel rooms quoted at US$ 100 cost approximately LE 330 or £60. At the other end of the scale a room in a three-star hotel may be US$ 30.00, LE 99 or £18. One and two-star hotels may be LE 20 or less. 12% service charge and small government and municipal taxes are added. All hotel meals are quoted in LE and are cheap.

If you choose one star hotels the room charge will be low and the cooking may be excellent. The rooms will be dusty but dust is endemic in Egypt: you have to get used to it. Mosquitoes will be more of a problem because smaller, cheaper hotels do not always have air conditioning or effective mosquito netting, but most now seem to have 'private facilities' in the shape of lavatory and shower.

Language — useful phrases

Hello   Ahlan

Good morning	Sabah el kheir
Good evening	Masaa el kheir
Please	Menfadelak
Thank you	Shoukran
Yes	Aywa
No	Laa
Excuse me	An iznak
After you	Itfadal
I want	Ayes
How much	Bikam
I don't have	Mafeesh
Almost	Yani
I do not want	Mish awiz
Where is the toilet?	Fain al-hammam
Airport	Matar
Street	Sharia
Square (in a town)	Midan
Railway	Seka hadid
Ticket	Tazkara
Coffee	Qahwa
Tea	Shai
Milk	Laban
Water	Maya
Bread	Eish
Butter	Zebda
Egg	Beid
Salt	Malh
Fruit	Fakha
Nice	Gamell
Bill	Fatoura
Money	Folous
Soap	Saboona

Lavatories

In some small hotels, lower grade restaurants, many offices and railway stations lavatories are apparently seldom cleaned and lavatory cisterns suffer from congenital paralysis. However the situation is much better than it was a few years ago (for example at airports) and is steadily improving. Remember that it is often possible to get some cleaning done. When viewing a room at a minor hotel look at the lavatory pan, and if necessary insist on its being cleaned as a condition of your staying there. When on a journey it is wise to take a small supply of toilet paper in your pocket because it is rarely, if ever, available in public lavatories.

Libraries

For English language books All Saints Episcopal Cathedral (behind the Marriott Hotel, Zamalek) has an excellent general library open daily except Friday. The British Council also has a library at 192 El Nil Street, Agouza, Cairo; tel. 345 3281/2. There is a French library at Madrasset El Huquq, El Frinseya, El Mounira; and the Library of Japanese Cultural Centre is at the Japanese Embassy, Cairo Centre Building 2, Abdel Keder, Hamza Street, Garden City, Cairo; tel. 355 3962.

Mosques

The most famous mosques in Cairo are the Al Azhar (the great university mosque) and the neighbouring Al Hussein mosque; the Mohamed Ali or Alabaster mosque in the Citadel; the Sultan Al Hassan mosque, the Refaie mosque, and Ahmed Ibn Tulun mosque, all in the Citadel area. Details in the Cairo chapter. Members of other faiths are usually allowed to visit mosques except at the times of regular prayer. However it is always advisable to ask first, before entering. Shoes must be removed and, though not always insisted upon, it is better for a woman to cover her head with a scarf or handkerchief. In some cases an entry charge is made. It is customary to tip the man who guards your shoes about 50 piastres.

Nile Cruises

For many people the initial vision of a holiday in Egypt is almost synonymous with a Nile cruise, and it is certainly the simplest as well as the most comfortable way of linking the areas of ancient Egypt: Cairo's pyramid district; Luxor and Aswan by way of the sites and temples that lie between. All these are described in the chapters on the Nile.

There are now more than 100 cruise ships on the Nile, indeed some of the old magic and peace has gone, because of the number of tourist craft plying up and down in the high season. However more and better boats are now available. The short, basic cruises are three to four days between Luxor and Aswan (the most interesting section of the river), and the passenger flies from Cairo to Luxor and back from Aswan to Cairo (or makes these journeys by train) or vice versa. Others sail from Cairo right up to Aswan. A few take their passengers on a full return trip, Cairo back to Cairo, taking about three weeks. Prices vary widely, but it must be noted that many cruises booked in Egypt are simply inclusive of the voyage; others include the connecting air or rail fares. Still others are part of a more comprehensive package holiday. For current prices contact the companies direct.

We list a few of the companies who operate the cruise ships:
Abercrombie and Kent (see Package Holidays) have their own luxury vessel 'Sun Boat' and also book cruises on Presidential, Oberoi and Sheraton ships.

Hilton Nile Cruises, Nile Hilton Hotel, Cairo; tel. 94260.
Oberoi Nile Cruises, Misr Travel Tower, Abassia, Cairo; tel. 836375.
Sheraton Nile Cruises, 48b Giza Street, Orman Building, Giza; tel.
348 5571/348 8215.

Package Holidays

Many companies organise package holidays to Egypt including:

Abercrombie and Kent, Sloane Square House, Holbein Place, London,
SW1W 8NS; tel. 071 730 9600/235 9761, offer several packages
including Cairo and Nile cruises; Upper Egypt by air; Alexandria
and El Alamein; Sinai/St Catherine; and safari holidays. Costs are
from £448 for four nights to £2057 for 15 nights.

Bales Tours Ltd, Bales House, Junction Road, Dorking, Surrey, RH4
3HB; tel. 0306 885991. Eight-day holidays from £455.

Thomas Cook Far Away Holidays, PO Box 36, Thorpe Wood,
Peterborough, PE3 6SB; tel. 0733 332255. Seven-day holidays from
£799; 14 days, including an 11-day Sheraton cruise, from £1099.

Hayes & Jarvis (Travel) Ltd, Hayes House, 152 King Street, London,
W6 0QU; tel. 081 748 5050, arrange a number of inexpensive
Egyptian holidays and cruises from £299.

Misr Travel is the tour operator owned by the Egyptian govern-
ment. It organises tours throughout Egypt, local excursions, etc.
London office: 201-204 Langham House, 308 Regent Street, London
W1R 5AL; tel. 071 255 1087.

Swan Hellenic, 77 New Oxford Street, London, WC1A 1PP; tel. 071
831 1515, offer Nile cruises of up to 17 days from Cairo to Aswan
from £1740 inclusive from London.

Thomson Worldwide, Holiday Shop, 4 Broadway, Five Ways,
Edgbaston, Birmingham, B15 1BB; tel. 021 632 6282. Seven-day
holidays from £325.

These prices quoted are for 1991 and should be checked before
future planning.

Photography

Egypt is a wonderful country for the photographer. First time visitors
should remember that the light is very strong, and that it is easy to
make errors of over-exposure. A light meter is useful and you will
need flash equipment for pictures inside temples and tombs. On
some archaeological sites a charge is made for the use of cameras

and cinecameras. In the Egyptian Antiquities Museum, the Islamic and the Coptic Museums in Cairo, the Graeco-Roman Museum in Alexandria and a few other places photography is not allowed except by special permit.

Never photograph local people without asking their permission, and approach them with courtesy. In some tourist centres they are eager to pose, and naturally expect *baksheesh*.

Public Holidays

National Holidays: May 1, May Day; July 26, Anniversary of the Egyptian Revolution; October 6, Egyptian Military Forces Day. Sham en Nessim is 'Easter Monday', the first Monday following the Coptic Easter which, like the Orthodox, differs from that of the western churches, but is usually within a week or two of the western date.

There are several Islamic festivals, the dates of which change as they are calculated by the lunar calendar. Several are associated with the fast of Ramadan, which in 1992 will start about the end of the first week in March and lasts for 30 days. It ends with the Id al Fitr holiday. This is followed 70 days later by Id al Adha, both holidays when all offices are closed for several days. Work continues during Ramadan itself, but not at high pressure as all practising Moslems fast from sunrise to sunset.

Shopping

Holiday or souvenir shoppers will find a rich field in cotton goods such as men's and women's galebeahs — the long, loose, all-enveloping garment worn by all Egyptians who have not adopted European dress — and tablecloths or dress lengths. There are also carvings, brass and leatherwork, some lovely costume jewellery and various other things like pottery and pictures painted on papyrus. In the souks or markets of any town you will be expected to bargain, and should aim to get the price down to near half the original offer. There are, however, tourist shops in Cairo, Luxor, Aswan and Alexandria where you can buy at fixed prices.

Shops are open 0900-2100 daily except Fridays. During Ramadan shopping hours vary.

Sport

Mild winter weather in Cairo and Alexandria gives opportunity for most outdoor sports. Winter resorts on the Red Sea and Gulf of Aqaba are outstanding for scuba-diving. Sandy beaches on the Mediterranean coasts offer swimming and water sports in summer.

Sporting Clubs

All Egypt's sporting clubs offer temporary membership to tourists. Several major hotels also arrange for their guests to use these facilities for a daily nominal fee.

Clubs: Gezira Sporting Club, Zamalek; Heliopolis Sporting Club, Heliopolis; Maadi Sporting and Yacht Club; Equestrian Club, Zamalek; Shooting Club, Dokki. Sports available include duck shooting at Fayoum; golf at the Gezira Sporting Club, the Mena House Oberoi Hotel and the Semouha Sporting Club, Alexandria; riding at stables near the Pyramids; rowing at the Egyptian Rowing Club near Cairo, and at the Sheraton Hotel; sailing at Cairo Yacht Club and at the Alexandria Yacht Club; scuba-diving at various resorts (see details in later chapters); tennis at the principal sporting clubs.

Telephones

Egypt's telephone system is now quite good and reliable. There are now some public coin-operated telephones (for example in Tahrir Square) and some hotels have automatic coin operated ones, the basic charge being 10 piastres for a local call. Shops will usually allow you to use their telephone for 10 piastres. Many hotels have telephones in the bedrooms: when this is the case, there should be no problem in making calls.

Time

The time in Egypt is two hours ahead of GMT. In summer clocks are advanced one hour.

Tipping

This is an essential part of life in Egypt, and the visitor must not be embarrassed by it, any more than the recipients are! It is very rare for an Egyptian to refuse a tip, though I have known it, and of course one must develop a sense of who is tippable and who is not. Most hotels add service charges as well as tax to the bill, so it is the extra, casual tipping for which one must be ready.

Here 'little and often' is the popular form. Two and sometimes three men may show you to your hotel room: one to carry the key, the others dividing the luggage. Each expects something. So do lift boys, doormen and so on: 50 piastres is ample for them. Even 20 piastres can be given to someone who hangs about having done nothing. The main difficulty is to have a constant supply of small change. Hotels cashiers have developed a trick of giving nothing smaller than 25 piastre notes, so it is often necessary to go to a bank to get small notes or coin.

Tourist Friends Association

This is an interesting organisation founded many years ago by the late General Mohamed Fouly, a general of police who retired from the service to devote all his time to the Tourist Friends. It is an entirely voluntary organisation which now has some 8,000 members in Cairo, and branches are being built up in other governorates. The idea is to develop real friendship and understanding between Egyptians and foreigners who visit the country. No payments are incurred. If you are a doctor, nurse, engineer, teacher, farmer or simply a home maker, and want to meet an Egyptian who follows the same calling — and can speak some English — the TFA will arrange it for you. Probably you will be asked to an Egyptian home and entertained to some simple hospitality: tea or coffee. If you want a companion to accompany you in Cairo (but not of course to compete with professional guides), again they will help you.

For anyone with a little time to spare in Egypt and a real wish to know the country and its people, the TFA is the gateway to many friendships. Write direct to the President: Col. Ahmed Fouly (son of the founder) TFA 9th Floor, 33 Kasr El Nil Street, Cairo; tel. 392 2036. Office open daily except Friday 1700-2000.

Tourist Offices

Abroad

London: Egyptian Tourist Authority, 168 Piccadilly, W1; tel. 071 493 5282/3.
New York: Egyptian Tourist Authority, 630 Fifth Avenue, New York 10111; tel. (212) 246 6960.
San Francisco: Egyptian Tourist Authority, 323 Geary Street, Suite 303, San Francisco, California 94102; tel. (415) 781 7676/7.
Tokyo: Egyptian Tourist Authority, Akasata 2 — Chome Annex, 2F, 19-8 Akasata 2 Chome Minato-Ku, Tokyo; tel. 589 0653.

In Egypt

Cairo: 5, Adly Street; tel. 3913454 (also at Cairo Airport tel. 667475).
Alexandria: Saad Zaghlul; tel. 807985.
Luxor: Tourist Bazaar; tel. 383294.
Aswan: Tourist Bazaar; tel. 32 32 97.
Port Said: Palestine Street; tel. 223 868.

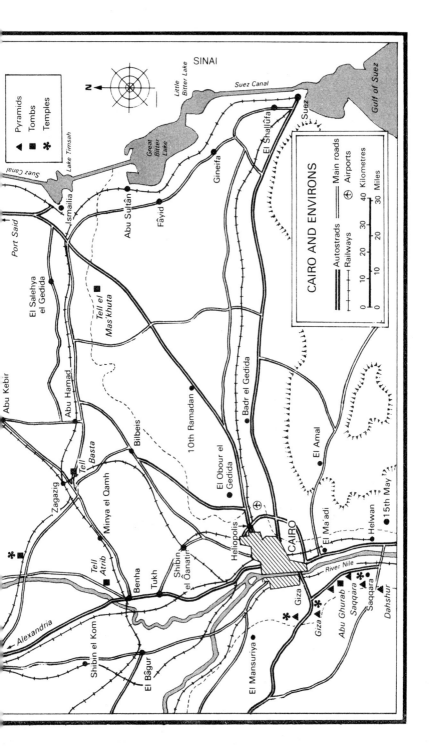

The Great Pyramid, Giza

History

Not unnaturally, Egypt's history is often thought of as concerning only the great days of the pharaohs, the chronicles of 30 dynasties recorded for us in hieroglyphs and temples and tombs which defy time beside the waters of the Nile.

Egyptian guides and even archaeologists are apt to mourn as decadent the introduction of first the Greek and then the Roman art styles and culture. To them the glory that was Egypt is an unique heritage, never shared and scarcely equalled by any other land. But the traveller with eyes to see and a mind to learn will find that this land later had a much more full and varied history, even though less rich and powerful. All the changing patterns of humanity in the Middle East, Africa and round the Mediterranean shores have passed over this country. Races have come and gone, leaving their features in its people, their thoughts and habits in the way of life. There have been ups and downs, times of great power and dominion and of decline, but Egypt's history is a living and continuing fact, not embalmed with its noble dead of 3 or 4,000 years ago.

Far back in prehistory, scholars have shown that this land of the Nile Valley was green, with forests and abundant animal life, inhabited by early man. But what happened to those people is a mystery still. The climate changed, the land became desert and the inhabitants vanished.

Ancient Egyptians
The ancient Egyptians as we know of them were not indigenous. They came northwards out of central Africa, or from the Libyan desert to the west or from Arabia — or there were migrations from all three areas which eventually merged into a recognisable Egyptian people, perhaps even before 10000 BC. By 4000 BC there were the cultures of Der Tasa and Badari in Upper Egypt (extending from Cairo to the Sudan border), and in Lower Egypt (the Cairo region, Delta and Mediterranean coast), that of Merimdah in the West Delta. Seven hundred years later, the peasant culture of Ma'adi which showed signs of Asiatic influence, was well established in the Cairo area.

Two separate kingdoms developed: the Red Kingdom in the north, named after the colour of the Nile mud in the Delta, and the White Kingdom of the south which extended to the first cataract near Aswan. About 3000 BC these kingdoms were united by the Upper Egyptian kings who subdued the north-western Delta state. After this, between 2950–2677 BC came the 1st and 2nd Dynasties with royal tombs at Abydos and the foundation of Memphis as capital. After the unification the tall, pepperpot-like 'white crown' and the 'red crown' — more like a helmet but with a high back and great projecting antenna — were combined, the white within the red, to form the double crown which is such a familiar part of the statues of the great pharaohs.

Old Kingdom
About 2676 BC came the 3rd Dynasty and what came to be known as the Old Kingdom. This was when the earliest known pyramid, the Step Pyramid at Saqqara, was built by Imhotep, high priest of Heliopolis. The century between 2620–2520 BC was the time of the 4th Dynasty and also the great period of pyramid building by Snofru, Cheops, Chephren and Mycerinus.

Four more dynasties followed until about 2200 BC when the Old Kingdom collapsed due to an influx of Asian peoples and local unrest. For the next 200 years there was an intermediate period during which the 11th Dynasty established its capital much farther south at Thebes (now Luxor).

Middle Kingdom
By the 12th Dynasty (1991–1786 BC) the Middle Kingdom came into being and its power spread still farther south with the conquest of Nubia; but this power too decayed, and by c1700 BC the whole area was dominated by the Asiatic Hyksos in the Delta region, with Avaris as its capital. Little more than a 100 years later, the kings of

27

History

the 17th Dynasty carried out the liberation of Egypt from Thebes; it was completed by the final conquest of the Hyksos by Ahmose (1568–1545 BC), founder of the 18th Dynasty.

New Kingdom

The New Kingdom and empire then established lasted for some 500 years and three dynasties, and its pharaohs included many of those whose names and achievements are most famous. Among them was Tuthmosis I (1524–1507 BC) whose armies advanced to the Euphrates and Hatshepsut (1503–1483 BC), the first queen to assume kingship and the status of god which went with it. The daughter of Tuthmosis, she was married to her half brother Tuthmosis II and at his death she established herself first as regent for another half brother Tuthmosis III and then declared herself pharaoh. For some 20 years she ruled, keeping Tuthmosis III in the background, building the great temple of Deir el Bahari on the west bank of the Nile at Thebes and bringing trees from far away Punt on the Red Sea to adorn it. In Thebes itself she set up a great granite obelisk. All pharaohs sought to outdo their predecessors in honouring the gods and their own memory, and Hatshepsut certainly established her place among them. She was evidently bitterly resented by Tuthmosis III for at her death he had her name removed from all the monuments she had created, and notably from her mortuary temple at Deir el Bahari.

Tuthmosis III became the great conquering general among pharaohs, sometimes called the Napoleon of the ancients, and in his time Egypt's lands extended from the Euphrates to the Sudan. This empire survived for another century after his death (c1449 BC).

Gods

The next outstanding event was a religious revolution. The early gods of the Egyptians took the form of animals, but greater than these was the sun god Re or Ra, worshipped in a city of the Delta called On and later known to the Greeks as Heliopolis. Up the Nile at Edfu, the sun god was called Horus and was represented as a hawk or falcon. The change from night to day was symbolised by the sun being reborn as a child, the arc of the night sky being the mother that gave him birth. Sometimes the sky was represented as a cow, and the new born god a calf.

As early as the 1st Dynasty, the gods were considered to have human characteristics and form except that they retained the head of the original sacred animal or bird — which is why one finds in the temple carvings and paintings Hathor, goddess of love and childbirth, with cow's horns, Anubis with a jackal's head, Horus that of a falcon, and so on.

Isis and Osiris are probably the most familiar Egyptian gods to western minds. They were two of the four children of Keb and Nut who in turn had been begotten by the sun god. Osiris ruled with his sister-wife Isis but was murdered and cut into many pieces by his brother Set. Isis in her sorrow sought these pieces throughout the world and eventually having recovered them all, revived Osiris by her magic, but he could not return to earth and so ruled as God of the underworld, while their son Horus reigned on earth and avenged his father on the evil Set.

Here came the pharaohs' identification with the gods. Every pharaoh ruled as Horus in his life on earth, and after death became Osiris who, with a company of judges representing the provinces of the land of Egypt, judged the dead as they passed through the underworld.

The whole galaxy of Egyptian gods and goddesses is a complex one, but the cult of Osiris has been called the most basic and consistent theme of Egyptian history. It became a kind of trinity: Osiris father and judge, Isis faithful wife and mother, and Horus (originally the sun god himself) the good son and inheritor. It was this trinity, under the embracing name of Amun that was worshipped at the great city of Thebes, and with which each pharaoh in his divinity was linked.

Pharaohs
There were four pharaohs of the 18th Dynasty named Amenhotep ('Amun is content') but it was the last of these, C1377–1360 BC, who proclaimed a new religion, the worship of a single universal god present in all life whom he called Aton. The king changed his own name to Akhenaton ('serviceable to Aton'), swept away the polytheism of the ancient temples, the system of priests, and eventually left Thebes and moved his capital to a town near the present Minya.

In a few short years the whole religious and constitutional life of a highly civilised country had been overturned by a sickly, ascetic man with a long thin rather unpleasant face which gazes enigmatically down from the walls of Luxor Museum and elsewhere on us today. He has another claim to fame: his wife was the beautiful Nefertiti whose sculptured head reproduced the world over is now in Berlin.

Akhenaton's gospel was short lived. After his death he was followed first and very briefly by his son-in-law and then by a half brother Tutankhaton, then only a boy of nine, who three years later restored Egypt to her ancient gods under the influence of the priests, and changed his own name to honour Amun. He died young, probably no more than 18 years old, but we know him as Tutankhamun, famous because he is the only pharaoh whose tomb was discovered

History

intact in Luxor's Valley of Kings, and so he is our initiator into the glories of ancient Egypt.

The religious revolution of Akhenaton was a strange episode in the history of Egypt, and one which still produces contrasting and strongly held views. There are those who see it as the first proclamation there of a monotheist religion, faith in a universal and loving creator. Modern Egyptian travel posters proclaim this. Others see it as a brief aberration in the classical splendour of ancient Egypt.

After that came the peak of the age of pharaohs, the 19th and 20th Dynasties which between 1317–1085 BC included the 67 year reign of Ramesses II — the 'King of kings'. There were 11 kings bearing the name of Ramesses and by the end of their reign their greatness was in decline, and the New Kingdom ended. Seven hundred and fifty years and 10 more dynasties came and went with kings of Libyan blood, Ethiopians and Persians, until the conquest of Alexander the Great in 332 BC.

Ptolemaic Dynasty
Alexander left Ptolemy to govern the country, who after Alexander's death, established a Ptolemaic dynasty, of whom Cleopatra of world fame was the seventh queen to bear that name. The Romans came in 30 BC, took the country as the personal property of the emperor and proceeded to grow wheat in vast quantities so that Egypt came to be known as the bread basket of the empire.

Christianity and Islam
Within the Roman period Christianity came, and the Coptic Church, one of the earliest churches, was established with Alexandria as its centre. Then in AD 641, only a few years after Mohamed proclaimed the Islamic faith, the Arabs conquered the country at the beginning of their triumphal advance westwards across North Africa and into Spain. Two Islamic dynasties the Fatimids and Ayyubids ruled Egypt between 969 and 1245, after which the Mameluks came to power. They were descended from Turkish stock, mercenaries who grasped control and ruled the country until it was conquered by the even more ruthless Ottoman Turks in the 16th century.

18th Century
By the late 18th century the French and English came into the picture. Napoleon occupied Egypt in 1798. Although he had to withdraw and suffered a naval defeat off Abukir (the Battle of the Nile) at the hands of Nelson, Napoleon introduced French scholars as well as soldiers, and the close connection of French archaeologists with the study and excavation of ancient Egypt started at that time. Indeed one Frenchman, Jean-François Champollion, unlocked the mystery of the Egyptian hieroglyphic inscriptions with his studies

started from the trilingual texts carved on the Rosetta stone found at Rosetta in the Nile Delta.

19th Century
In 1805 a young Albanian-born officer, Mohamed Ali, was elected Pasha (hereditary ruler) by the Sheikhs of Cairo and confirmed in office by the Turkish Sultan. He established a dynasty which only ended with Farouk's abdication in 1952. It was Mohamed Ali who began the modernisation of Egypt.

In 1856 Vicomte Ferdinand de Lesseps, the French scientist and diplomat, was invited by the ruler, Said, to start work on the Suez Canal, which was finally opened in 1869. Britain's fast route to India and the East was realised via this new waterway. Under the agreement which was signed in 1882, Britain gained control over the Suez Canal for 99 years.

20th Century
Turkey's rule over Egypt ended when Britain declared it a protectorate during the 1914–18 war and this continued until 1936, though provisions for a constitutional monarchy were drawn up after the war in 1922. By the time the protectorate ended in 1936, war clouds were again gathering and Britain undertook the defence of Egypt, when it was invaded by the Germans and Italians who were defeated by the British Eighth Army at El Alamein in 1942.

Ten years later, a bloodless army coup overthrew Farouk's government, and shortly afterwards brought Gamel Abdel Nasser to power. The nationalisation of the Suez Canal and demands for the withdrawal of British troops followed. This caused the joint British, French and Israeli attack on Egypt in 1956, an event which came to be known as the Suez Crisis. After Nasser's death in December 1970, Anwar Sadat became President. A permanent constitution was drawn up and came into operation in 1971. The President is nominated for a period of six years and is eligible for unlimited renomination. He is Chief of State, Head of Government and Supreme Commander of the Armed Forces: he appoints a Vice President, Prime Minister, government ministers etc. There is also a Consultative Assembly and a People's Assembly.

Today there are four main political parties, the ruling National Democratic Party, the Socialist Workers' Party (the official opposition), the Liberal Socialist Party and the Unionist Progressive Party.

During the Six Day War of 1967, the Israelis occupied the Sinai peninsula. In the countering war of October 1973, Egypt regained the Suez Canal and its sense of national honour. By this time, President Sadat had gained a memorable if controversial place on the world stage. In 1972, he dispensed with the Soviet presence in

History

his country and in 1977 he made his historic peace visit to Israel which resulted in the return of Egypt's Sinai territory and badly needed oilfields. In 1978 he was awarded a Nobel Peace Prize. Despite Anwar Sadat's continued championship of the Palestinian cause, the price of Egypt's own success was hostility from the rest of the Arab world and his assassination by Moslem extremists on October 6 1981 was a traumatic event in Middle East politics and modern history.

After the death of Sadat, Hosni Mubarak, who had served as Vice-President to Sadat since 1975, was appointed President. He had previously played a prominent part in the planning of the 1973 war and was formerly Commander in Chief of the Air Force. In April 1982 the last section of occupied Sinai was restored to Egypt, and Mubarak has taken as his mission the mending of relations with other Arab states while retaining understanding with Israel. During the Gulf War of 1991, Egypt was a leading nation in the Alliance which liberated Kuwait.

Statue of Ramesses II at Saqqara

Right: *the Sphinx at Giza. Abercrombie & Kent*
           Galebeahs for sale outside Habu Medinet
           Hutchison Library
Overleaf: *The Alabaster Mosque, Cairo*
           Sunboat I on the Nile, Abercrombie &
           Kent

Typical Egyptian Shop

The People

In paintings on the walls of tombs, temple carvings, triumphant statuary or mummy cases there is a face which we may take to be the likeness of the typical ancient Egyptian man. Except where this is clearly a personal portrait, as in representations of Akhenaton and some other celebrities, the characteristics are the same whether they portray a pharaoh, a priest or a procession of anonymous soldiers, servants or fishermen. The physique is slight but well built, the features — faces are always shown in profile — fine drawn with a thin straight nose and enormous almond shaped eyes; these eyes are the dominant and most memorable features.

For years I believed that this face, familiar to anyone who has studied reproductions of early Egyptian paintings was an art style rather than genuine likeness. Not for one moment did I believe that people, lots of people, really had eyes like that. Then one day some years ago when I made my first visit to the tombs at Saqqara I met

Previous page: *Qait Bey Fort, Alexandria*
                     Felluccas on the Nile, Abercrombie & Kent
Left: *Tombs of the Nobles, Thebes*
                     Columns at Karnak

The People

a living example of the ancient Egyptian. He was a tall, slim young man wearing the ubiquitous long white galebeah and he was one of the official custodians of the tombs and the great necropolis of mummified bulls. Here were those extraordinary eyes, the delicate nose, the face that is neither Arab nor African as we know them, but was apparently the typical Egyptian of four or five thousand years ago. These people, often of the Nile villages, are usually Copts, for the simple reason that Egypt's ancient Christian minority has not intermarried with the subsequent conquerors and immigrants.

A link in this chain between the ancient dynasties and our own time is shown by some of the later mummies of the Roman period when a fashion came in for placing a painting of the dead person's face over the head of the mummy. There are examples in both Cairo's Antiquities Museum and the Graeco-Roman Museum at Alexandria which show the distinctive eyes and nose very clearly. The people of Egypt are the true and living identity of the country, and they are very varied, which is what gives the Egypt of today its perennial interest and vitality.

Individuals travel for a variety of reasons — climate, relaxation, sport, scenery, archaeology, art, but also to see and know people. With a country like Egypt there is so famous a heritage of ancient culture and dramatic scenery that many will come and go satisfied with these alone. When that is the case I think they will mostly leave at the end, content to have seen and not to return. In a lifetime of travel I have known many countries which I visited with interest but unless I found and was found by the people I had no urge to come back. Where the bonds of friendship and understanding were established I returned rejoicing, as often as I could. That, I think, is the true meaning of travel as it is perhaps the essential difference between being a traveller and a tourist.

There is of course no typical Egyptian, any more than there is a typical Englishman, Irishman, Welshman or Scot. The overall likeness is only apparent from a distance. History has shown that there was no known link between prehistoric man and those long-eyed people of the River who have persisted through the millennia. But in any case they are only a minority now.

Through the centuries, races from every direction have come to make up what is now the Egyptian people: nomads from the great Libyan deserts, sailors and fishermen from the Mediterranean littoral, farmers of the Nile Valley, Greek, Roman, Persian, tall, black, fine-featured Nubians from the south, tribes from the deep heart of Africa, Arabs, Turks and others from Asia Minor.

One can see traces of most of them in the jostling crowds of Cairo: tall, short, fat, laughing, imperturbable, neat and grizzled, calm and dignified, light-skinned or dark, pretty importunate children, cheeky students, courteous officials, elegant modern women.

What binds together the majority of Egyptians is their religion. Egypt is an Islamic country, though with a large Christian minority which has been estimated at between 10 and 20 per cent, the importance of which must not be ignored.

The peoples of this land seem always to have been of a strongly religious character whatever their origin. The ancient Egyptians worshipped primitive gods but raised those gods and their cults to high spiritual level. They were very deeply concerned with the after life, though the preparations which we can see that they made for it seem to have been mainly the continued provision of this world's goods. The Greeks and Romans brought their own gods, but as good colonists strove to identify these with the ancient gods of the country.

Coptic Church

Christianity is older than Islam, and the Coptic Church was one of the earliest of the Christian communities. It claims its foundation directly from St Mark, author of the earliest of the Synoptic Gospels, identified as a native of Cyrene in North Africa, who came to Alexandria in 61 AD where he preached and baptised. Thus the Coptic Church was born. The word 'Copt' originally simply meant Egyptian but in time came to be used specifically for a Christian Egyptian.

Seven years later, St Mark was martyred in the streets of Alexandria by fanatical followers of the Graeco-Egyptian god Serapis. Long afterwards in the 9th century his relics were carried away to the great basilica built in his honour in Venice, but in celebration of the nineteenth centenary of St Mark's martyrdom, Pope Paul VI of Rome returned the relics to the Coptic Church. They were received in 1968 by the Coptic Pope Kyrillos VI of Alexandria with great celebrations, in which the Coptic Emperor Haile Selassie of Ethiopia took part.

St Mark was the first of Egypt's Christian martyrs, but later there were many more, especially during the time of the emperor Diocletian when the number was estimated at 800,000 men, women and children. In the Roman Byzantine period the persecutions were declared official by imperial edict. With the coming of the Arabs the oppression ended, but persecutions continued through personal Islamic fanaticism until the wise rule of Mohamed Ali began in 1805.

Monasticism early became a special feature of the Coptic Church and monks and nuns who lived singly as hermits or in communities in the desert have always formed an important part of its life. There are many Coptic monasteries in different parts of the country and a number can be visited by special permission. Some are now experiencing a notable revival with many new entrants.

Islam

Wherever you go in Egypt you will find mosques: magnificent domed edifices with exquisite minarets, or humble buildings in a dirty back street, identifiable only by the shoes outside the doorway and a glimpse of the quiet, carpeted space within. Loudspeakers have, unhappily, taken over from the thin, haunting voice of the human muezzin, but the call is still made through town and village at the hours of prayer: dawn, noon, afternoon, sunset and at night.

Islam is a way of life, affecting laws, food, and all aspects of living, and, although not every Moslem is deeply devout, virtually everyone respects and, generally speaking, observes the rules of Islam in the way that Christian ethics and behaviour were accepted and honoured in Europe at least until the turn of the century. Many Moslems have a deep faith, and it is quite normal in a big luxury hotel to see the staff go in turn to a corner of the offices to stand and kneel while making their evening prayer.

Religious tolerance

Because of the natural simplicity and lack of embarrassment in this practice of religion — whether it is among Moslems or Christians, or no doubt among the remaining but small Jewish community — it is much easier for a believer to meet Egyptians on the level of personal friendship than for an atheist or agnostic to do so. There is a ready respect for belief, even of another faith. Indeed the Moslem will probably show more easy acceptance and respect for the thoughts of the western Christian than for his Coptic cousins because although there is official and general tolerance between the two religions, frictions tend to arise over such matters as marriage and property. If one enjoys philosophical discussion, Egyptians are very interesting companions. The Tourist Friends Association — see General Information — can arrange meetings.

Most short term holidaymakers, of course, will have little chance to meet Egyptians except taxi drivers, shopkeepers, waiters or room boys, when conversation tends to have a financial bias. What is often overlooked is that thay are genuinely interested in strangers. There is a friendly curiosity at almost all the social levels. A single woman will receive romantic overtures from the most unlikely men; they are seldom difficult to restrain — if you want to, that is — and one should never react with anger! The simplest protection is to invent a husband and large family of children, preferably not too far away, if you do not happen to be endowed with them in fact, since all Egyptians love children.

Al Azhar Mosque

Cairo

The old adage about not being able to see the wood for the trees is particularly true of Cairo. Only from the top of the great Cairo Tower, a modern landmark which rises some 183 m (600 ft) from Gezira Island in the centre of the Nile, or from the Mokkatam Hills to the south east can one get any idea of the extent or form of Egypt's capital, the largest city in Africa with a population of 14 million.

Arriving from the airport, as most western visitors do, one comes by broad modern roads into the north east of the city and then through a network of streets and squares where the traffic becomes increasingly dense. Cars crawl and hoot, buses, donkey carts, cyclists and pedestrians form a human and architectural maze in which it is easy to lose all sense of direction and probably the last remnants of travel-weary patience. This is of course true of many other large cities, but Cairo is a confusing place and few will bestow on it love at first sight. Do not judge it hastily: it is a seething living experience, not a planned entity.

The Nile, broad and majestic, flows through the heart of it, straddled by bridges and with two major islands, Gezira and Roda Islands at the heart of both river and city. The Nile is Cairo's life blood and its

41

beauty, especially at night when lights twinkle above it and are reflected in the dark waters. The skyline of the town has its own magic
too, most evocative at dawn or sunset: a forest of minarets, domes
and spires, the mosques and churches rising above the streets and
shops, together with a number of modern high-rise buildings which
have their own dignity. But all this one discovers later.

History

Cairo is very ancient, though the great capitals of the pharaonic
period were not here but farther south, at Memphis and Thebes.
The origins of Cairo go back about 4,500 years to a city north-east
of the present centre which was called On, and renamed Heliopolis,
city of the sun, by the Greeks and later the Romans because it was
always a place of sun worship. It was mainly foreign conquerors
who chose this as their metropolis because it was the natural
centre between the fertile Delta and Upper Egypt, and near to their
entry points to the country — by the land route from Arabia and by
the Mediterranean shores, whereas the ancient Egyptians based
their power in Upper Egypt and the borders of Nubia.

When the Persians arrived between 500 and 400 BC, their emperor
Cambyses chose to establish a city which became known as
'Babylon', where the district of Old Cairo now stands. Alexander
the Great created Alexandria on the coast, but succeeding Greeks
and Romans still honoured Heliopolis, and when the Arabs arrived
what is now Cairo became first a military camp and then a city
named Fustat. This has remained the national capital and the centre
of life, administration, Islamic study and trade, though it is to the
Fatimids, who came to Egypt in 969 AD that the real foundation of
Islamic Cairo is credited. Their commander Jawhar Al-Saqally
ordered a new town to be built both as a military base and an
official residence for the caliphate. At the time the planet Mars,
called in Arabic Al-Qahir, was in the ascendant, and this name was
chosen for the city. The modern name of Cairo is derived from this.

Gezira and Roda Islands

The river Nile flows northwards through the city and dividing its
waters in the northern metropolitan section is the long island of
Gezira with the Cairo Tower towards its southern end, standing
between the National Sporting Club and the grounds of the famous
Gezira Sporting Club. The Tower has two storeys at the top, one
with a revolving floor and there is a restaurant and cafeteria.
'Panoramic equipment' is provided at the top to aid the visitor on
locating the principal sights. Close by is the magnificent new Cairo
Opera House, a gift of the Japanese Government, opened in 1988,
where musical and dance seasons are given in winter.

North of that is a residential district called Zamalek with a number of embassies. Zamalek has a peaceful charm and dignity, and in some ways is the Kensington of Cairo; the new Episcopal (Anglican) cathedral is here, immediately behind the Marriott Hotel.

Gezira is a lovely area with trees and gardens, pleasant to wander in if time allows. You will cross this island continually during any stay in Cairo for three major streets (26th July Street, 6th October Street and Al Tahrir Street) pass through it, linked by matching bridges to the east and west banks.

Sixth October Bridge passes the Cairo Tower and continues to the east as a flyover for some distance, eventually leading to Ramesses Square and the railway station. Al Tahrir Street crosses to the southern end of Gezira and leads to Tahrir Square.

Immediately south of Gezira Island is Roda Island which is almost entirely covered with streets, houses, shops, mosques and with the Nilometer at its southern or upstream tip. The Nilometer (a graduated pillar — the system used by ancient Egyptians to show the heights to which the Nile rose during the annual floods) is believed to date from 715 AD.

East Bank

On the section of the east bank near Tahrir Bridge you are in the administrative, business and social centre of Cairo. Here are several of the leading hotels such as the Ramesses Hilton, Nile Hilton, Semiramis, Shepheard's and Meridien, as well as many less exclusive ones, and it is the area where many visitors will stay during their time in Cairo. On this side Tahrir Bridge leads on to Midan Tahrir (Liberation Square) which is a hub for most of the city routes, a notorious place for traffic jams. There are steps and overhead walkways for pedestrians to reach the different streets which fan out from it. One is Talaat Harb Street which leads to Talaat Harb Square where it is crossed by Kasr el Nil Street; these are two of the smart shopping streets of Cairo.

Beyond this to the east are more streets of shops, offices and banks and eventually the district of the Al Azhar mosque, a number of other famous mosques and the well known bazaar area — the Khan el Khalili souk.

Just north of Tahrir Square is the great Egyptian Antiquities Museum, and to its south the Garden City. Some distance due east of this section lies the Citadel with another group of famous mosques, and a road leading up to the Mokkatam Hills with a fine view westwards across the Nile to the Pyramids.

Opposite the southernmost tip of Roda Island, on the eastern bank but just inland from the river, is the quarter known as Old Cairo, the principal centre for ancient Coptic churches, the earliest Jewish synagogue and the Coptic Museum; all of which stand approximately where the Persians' 'Babylon' was built.

West Bank

On the west bank of the Nile there is a corniche road along the river with more hotels, of which the Cairo Sheraton is probably the best known. The western end of 6th October Bridge across Gezira Island leads to the big Agricultural Museum and farther up, opposite Roda Island, are the beautiful grounds of the Zoological Garden where there is a fine collection of animals from Egypt and the Sudan.

Just south of this is the Cairo district known as Giza and the roads leading out of the city to the Giza Pyramids which are about 15 km (9 miles) away, and on to Upper Egypt as well as northwards to Alexandria.

Exploring the City
As far as the visitor is concerned there are, therefore, some five districts to explore within the city itself; first the Tahrir Square quarter and the Garden City; secondly, Al Azhar; thirdly, the Citadel and Mokkatam Hills; fourth, Old Cairo; and lastly, as described above, Gezira Island and the Zoological Garden — Giza district. Of these districts, the first four are undoubtedly tourist highlights.

The next step is to decide how to see them. Time will be the controlling factor. If you can give a complete week to Cairo alone there will be no problems. Devote a day to each area, and you can probably include the Pyramids and Sphinx with the city part of Giza. If there are only a couple of days available then you must be selective.

Guided Tours

In any case, a half-day conducted sightseeing tour is a good introduction to any city, and will be time and money well spent in a place as varied and confusing as Cairo. A number of companies organise these trips including Misr Travel, (see General Information). There are, for example, half day trips which visit the Egyptian Museum and then provide a general 'orientation' tour of the centre of the city. There are also many other trips devoted to the districts I have mentioned and sometimes combining two such areas. These are best booked through the hotel where you are staying — all sizeable hotels do this — unless such sightseeing is already scheduled in your inclusive holiday.

Alternatively you can hire a personal guide and tell him what you want to see, doing the tour in a hire car. This is of course more expensive than a bus tour, but many of the organised tours are by car for a given number of people. Guides with or without cars are hired through the travel agencies; the principal ones have offices in or attached to the major hotels.

As with the inclusive holiday packages there is a good deal to be said for taking a trained guide. There are still a few of the traditional dragomen who wear the flowing galebeah and turban, giving the impression that you are seeing Cairo as did the leisurely travellers at the turn of the century. All reputable guides obtained through a regular agency are knowledgeable, though some of the history and anecdotes they recount may not be wholly reliable. Many holiday-makers are not unduly troubled by this: but the interested visitor will want to ask questions, and only the really knowledgeable guide with qualifications will be able to give you satisfactory replies.

There remains the intrepid traveller's method of exploring independently. This for many people is much more fun, though to be honest you can miss a lot unless you have done a great deal of homework in advance about the things and places to see. The best way to see and explore a city is always on foot, and much of the centre of Cairo can be covered in this way, but it is a big city, so you will need to take taxis part of the time.

Public Transport
The final sign of the initiated is to be able to use local buses and trams, but I would not recommend this until you at least know Cairo reasonably well or speak some Arabic. At the busy times of day the buses are crammed to overflowing. Fares are only a few piastres but the main problem for the stranger is to discover which buses go where, and the points at which to get on or off. The new underground is excellent, but at present there is only one line which starts at El Marg in the NE and runs right through, linking the main railway station, Tahrir Square and Old Cairo, to Helwan in the south, 32 stations in all.

It is standard advice to agree a price with a taxi driver before starting the journey, and you should try to get down to about two-thirds of the original asking price. If you want a taxi to take you to a lesser known destination or a private address you may have difficulty. Cairo drivers are not so omniscient as London cabbies, and they do not speak much English (see General Information).

When one has sufficient time to ramble, it is an idea to take a taxi to the furthest point of your morning's excursion and to walk back with the aid of a map. When you have done this once or twice successfully you will have begun to be at home in Cairo, and then you are not very far from loving it.

Cairo

On one visit I took a taxi from Shepheard's Hotel to the Coptic Museum in Old Cairo — about a 15 minute drive. I walked back, and when I reached the Nile corniche opposite Roda Island, a herd of camels was being driven smartly over the Al Mlek al Saleh Bridge and down the street to meet me! There must have been 60 or 70 of them, beautiful young animals, branded on the side with the owner's mark like English sheep. One man rode at their head, another ran breathless behind them and they came through the heart of Cairo at a gallop, towering above the puny cars. Crossing onto the river side of the street I then walked quietly back, northwards to my hotel. Several barbers had brought out wooden chairs and little cases of instruments and were busily shaving their customers there under the trees beside the river, while farther on a woman beggar was timidly approaching the few passers-by till the midday call of the muezzin sounded over the water.

Egyptian Museum

Whether you enjoy museums or not, the great Egyptian Museum which stands just to the north of Tahrir Square is virtually obligatory for all visitors. Here are most of the treasures of ancient Egypt which have been found by archaeologists up and down the country. Those that were not carried off to the great collections in London, Berlin and elsewhere, that is. Egyptians not unnaturally still feel defrauded by the removal of some of their historic heritage, but to be honest the early archaeologists and most of the money to support their excavations came from other countries and it would be strange if they had left all their discoveries behind at a time when public opinion was less democratically altruistic than it claims to be now.

Nonetheless, priceless treasures remain and as far as the pharaonic time is concerned they are gathered here, apart from the fine collection in Alexandria and some smaller local museums. For most visitors the chief attraction is the special collection from Tutankhamun's tomb. There are chairs and beds and chariots, jewels and the strangely evocative collection of fruits and seeds which were buried with the king to provide food for the journey and a means of sowing crops in the next world: dates and grapes and barley, with leaves and fruit from the sacred persea tree.

All this is on the upper floor of the museum. Below are major carvings, tombs and huge works in stone or marble. Everyone who comes here several times will have their own favourite exhibits. Mine are the wax paintings on wood or linen which provided a likeness of the deceased and were placed over the wrappings covering the face of a mummy in the 2nd centry AD. I have mentioned these when writing on the features of the early Egyptians and there is a fine collection of such paintings in room 14.

The catalogue is a mixed blessing. Most of the exhibits are moved about from time to time and although numbered it is almost impossible to match the exhibit with the entry or vice versa. Still, some information is given (in English) beside most objects. If you go round with a guide they will of course point out the most important things. A quick circuit of the museum can be made in one hour; in two you can see most of the best of it. The entrance fee is LE 10.

Shops

If you are staying in this area the museum is an excellent focal point for an afternoon spent on foot. After so much culture one can cross the meeting place of streets and tramways which lies just to the left of the front of the museum and wander up Kasr el Nil Street to look at the shops. Cairo shops are small and not very impressive when compared with European capitals, but here and in the neighbouring Talaat Harb Street there are jewellers, shoe shops (prices often less than half those in London), handbags and other leatherware, flowers, photographers and bookshops. Tea at Groppi's is a link with the past and always enjoyable. Choose your pastry in the entrance shop as you go in.

Garden City

By turning right out of the continuation of Kasr el Nil Street and keeping more or less due south through a network of small streets you will come in 20 or 30 minutes — depending on how slowly you wander and how many times you lose direction — to the back of the Garden City area. The walk is a vivid example of the contrasts of Cairo. You are within a square mile which contains the great buildings of the National Assembly, the Egyptian Museum, the Hilton Hotels and several of the more important embassies but here you will find some of the smaller everyday souks where local people buy their goods. Goats amble about, one man wrings the necks of chickens as he takes them out of a stack of coops and others sit at their doors thoughtfully smoking hookahs. Comparatively few visitors seem to pass through these little streets, but no one minds your walking quietly along. It would be discourteous to stand and gape at what is unfamiliar to us: tourists are expected to gape, but they should confine this occupation to places like the Pyramids.

Coming to the back of the National Assembly you leave this teeming quarter for a more dignified one, usually rather empty and peaceful in the late afternoon, and here you can cut back towards the Nile. The British Embassy with its semicircle of gardens has the finest position in the Garden City overlooking the Nile. Almost immediately behind its discreet walls is the American Embassy and in the neighbouring streets there are others, as well as banks, insurance offices and the headquarters of various organisations.

Many of these are in graceful mansions built in the late 19th and early 20th centuries, legacies of 'colonial' Egypt. Some of those now used for offices have a rather sad, sleepy dignity; the days of their elegant parties are over, the buildings are shabby, their gardens neglected. The Garden City is a peaceful place in which to wander as the sun sinks westwards over the river.

The Al Azhar district

This is the heart of the first Islamic city of Cairo. Four years after the Fatimid commander Jawhar al-Saqally started on the new capital, the great mosque of Al Azhar was completed in AD 973. It has always been a seat of learning as well as a mosque, and is one of the oldest universities in the world. Many of the most famous Moslem scholars have studied there through the centuries. At first it was only a religious university, but later other faculties were added. The major part of this large Islamic University is now at Nasr City, a modern district of Cairo east of the Mokkatam Hills and south of Heliopolis.

More than a thousand years old, the great mosque with its halls and minarets has been extended over the years and it has a famous library with a priceless collection of books and manuscripts.

The part behind the large courtyard is the oldest section, and the prayer niche of Fatimid days has been retained. As in many less famous and ancient mosques perhaps the most impressive thing about the great, spacious carpeted interior is a reverential sense of peace. That, and the little groups of students who sit on the floor grouped round the chair of their lecturer. 'That is the origin of the "professorial chair," ' said a retired Egyptian general who was taking me round. I had never heard that before, but it could well be true. Students come in and out, very much at home, but always with a sense of respect. Often you will see them walking up and down or sitting on the floor, book in hand, their lips moving silently as they commit some passage to memory. Tourists are not usually admitted to Al Azhar in the mornings because it is a time of study, but groups of two or three may be allowed to enter.

There are so many mosques in this district that a forest of minarets seems to rise above the rooftops. Close by is the Al Hussein mosque, named after the grandson of the Prophet, which possesses some of the most sacred Islamic relics and is one of the great mosques for congregational worship in Cairo. Entrance is forbidden to non-Moslems. Another is the Al Hakim mosque, now partly ruined but dating from AD 1010.

Bazaar

After removing one's shoes continually to enter these mosques a return to the world of trade and barter may be a good contrast, and only a few minutes' walk from Al Azhar itself is the labyrinth of souks called Khan el Khalili which for some 600 years has been Cairo's principal bazaar. Do not go here early in the morning: at 10 o'clock you will find the traders just beginning to take down their shutters and put out their wares. Business starts in the late morning but continues into the evening and the most picturesque time to visit the souks is after sundown when the booths are brightly lit and the alleyways full of a seething crowd of people.

Here are jewellers and sellers of brass and leatherwork and the long, loose galebeahs worn by both men and women, though the style and colours differ for the sexes. This is the place to buy souvenirs and gifts of Egyptian workmanship. Some of the goods are shoddy and in execrable taste, others are really good. Many of the booths at the edge of the souk cater simply for the tourist. All guides will direct you to the popular type of tourist wares, and many will take you to those owned by their brothers or cousins who give them a commission on the business they bring.

You are expected to bargain, and should aim to get your purchases for about half the first asking price, although this is not often achieved. If you want to see the real local part of the souks you will have to press on past the trinkets and camel saddles and then — to the amazement and disappointment of the guide — you can find the spice and vegetable stalls, butchers and tailors and tinsmiths who make up the trading world of everyday Egyptian life. Incense is sold opposite the entrance of the Al Hussein mosque. As far as personal souvenir shopping is concerned the choice here will be wider, though you may drive better bargains in Luxor or some of the smaller towns.

This area must be explored on foot, though transport will probably be needed to get there and back.

The Citadel and Mokkatam Hills

Although not far from Al Azhar the places to visit here are separated by some distance and if one is going up to the hills, a car (or coach tour) is needed.

The Citadel (entrance fee LE 3) is an impressive fortress-like structure which was started in 1176 by Salah-el-Din (Saladin to the westerners) to dominate the city from the foothills of Mokkatam and finally completed in 1207. It includes the Mohamed Ali Mosque, also known as the Alabaster Mosque. This is one of the superb examples of Islamic architecture, though not an ancient one as it was built by the famous and much honoured Mohamed Ali in the early 19th century and is modelled on the Nur-ed-Din Mosque in Istanbul. He died in 1849 and his tomb is in the south-west corner and a place of veneration to many Moslems. There is a beautiful terrace with superb views of Cairo, and within the Citadel's walls are the Police Museum and the Military Museum.

Just north of the Citadel and below it is the Sultan Al-Hassan Mosque built in 1356, the largest mosque in Cairo and possessing the tallest minarets. It is one of the masterpieces of Islamic work in Egypt. Immediately opposite this is the Refaie Mosque, which is the mausoleum of the former Egyptian Royal Family; the tombs include that of King Fouad I and a sister of King Farouk. A short distance to the north you will find the Blue Mosque built in the 14th and restored in the 17th century.

Due west of the Citadel is the Ahmed Ibn Tulun Mosque. This has a huge open quadrangle surrounded by cloisters, and its broad paving stones have been restored. Built in AD 879 it is considered to be Cairo's oldest mosque because it has not been materially changed, although it was restored in 1296 when an Islamic school for study of the Koran, law and medicine was added.

One of the chief interests for the visitor is a museum in what was a private house virtually built into the outer walls of the mosque. In the 1920s a Major Gayer-Anderson bought and restored two houses built in the 17th century by one Hajj Mohamed al-Jazzar. He made one house out of them and lived there for many years, furnishing it with genuine old Egyptian furniture and treasures. At his death he bequeathed the building and its marvellous and very personal contents to the state. Do not miss the Anderson House, it is one of the most fascinating places in Cairo with its carved window screens, secret room and roof terraces.

If you take an organised tour which goes there, or have someone such as a reliable guide or knowledgeable friend to show you where to go, the tombs of the Mameluk caliphs in the huge graveyard called the City of the Dead below the Mokkatam Hills are interesting. From there, carry on up to the hills themselves to get a superb view — if the day is clear. Beyond this in the district called Nasr City is the handsome new Conference Centre where a number of international conferences have been held.

Old Cairo

Old Cairo, built on the foundations of the Persians' 'Babylon' and therefore first inhabited some 2,500 years ago is now the heart of the old Coptic Cairo. Proudly, the Coptic Church would view its first Christian initiation as before the coming of St Mark: citing the visit of the Holy Family when they fled to Egypt from Herod's persecution. Miracles are ascribed to the infant Jesus at various places in Egypt where the Holy Family is thought to have travelled before finally reaching 'Babylon'. The Coptic church of St Sergius was built in the 4th century over the site where they sheltered. Later the Holy Family is said to have travelled to Upper Egypt and a number of places are linked with these early Christian traditions.

The Romans built a fort in 'Babylon', parts of which remain, and above it a Coptic church was built dedicated to the Blessed Virgin, but more generally known as El Mouallaqa or the Hanging Church because it seems to be suspended over the fort. It is a beautiful and famous church in basilica form, and is the only one in Old Cairo which is completely without a dome — a normal feature of Coptic design. Details of the church and its icons are given in a booklet on sale in the church compiled by the local church education group and translated into English by a Coptic lady, Iris Habib el Masri who is an authority on Egyptian church history.

The Coptic Museum is beside the Hanging Church and has a comprehensive collection of Coptic exhibits. Next door to it is the Greek Orthodox church of St George and only a few minutes walk away is another Coptic church dedicated to St Barbara, a young Christian martyr, and built in the 5th century. There are said to be seven Coptic churches in this district but I have not traced them all. Here too is the oldest synagogue in Egypt, the synagogue of Ben Ezra, which traces its origins back to the visit of Rabbi Abraham Ben Ezra from Jerusalem in AD 1115. He visited the Christian Patriarch who then held the land where an earlier synagogue had stood and the site was restored to the Jewish community. A new synagogue named after Ben Ezra was built on this site. It is a quiet peaceful place with a small garden, behind the walls of Old Cairo's narrow alleys which have changed little since the Middle Ages.

Also in Old Cairo is the Episcopal (Anglican) church dedicated to Jesus, Light of the World. This was built as a memorial to Canon Temple Gairdner, Christian missionary and Arabist, who was greatly beloved and honoured in Cairo where he died in 1928. The congregation is almost entirely Egyptian and services are in Arabic. A school for deaf children is attached to the church.

Other places to visit

These areas and the places mentioned within them by no means exhaust the sights of Cairo. There are many other mosques and churches of different denominations including the Anglican cathedral. Museums are legion. Notable among them is the Museum of Islamic Art between the National Assembly and the Al Azhar region. This was founded by the Khedive Ismail in the mid-1800s and the collection originally housed in the Al-Hakim mosque was moved to the present building about 80 years ago. It is said to contain the most comprehensive collection of Islamic art in the world.

Others are the Agricultural Museum on the west bank; the Papyrus Institute, El Nil Street, Giza, near the Sheraton Hotel; the Modern Art Museum, Ismail Abul Fetouh Street, Dokki (also west bank); Egyptian Civilization and Gezira Museum on the Gezira exhibition ground; the Ethnological Museum, Kasr el Aini Street and the Geological Museum, 1 Sheikh Rihan Street.

Cairo University is situated on the west bank and the main entrance is opposite the Giza bridge from Roda Island. It numbers well over 100,000 students and is the largest higher education centre in the Middle East, to which students come from all over the Arab world. Its most famous faculties are those of medicine and engineering.

The American University, which is close to the American Embassy, is also well known, though much smaller. Four-fifths of the students are Egyptians, and it has an important Islamic Art and Architecture library.

The Pharaonic Village created by Dr Hassan Ragab of the Dr Ragab Papyrus Institute is on the west bank of the Nile almost opposite the Old Cairo area. This is well worth a half day visit — a village built entirely in ancient Egyptian form where about 300 people live and work with the tools of the ancients. You glide through these living tableaux in a boat, and can walk among them too. Entrance charge about LE 15.

Heliopolis of the ancients is now a residential area on the way to the airport and about 25 kilometres (15 miles) from the city centre. There is an obelisk, the only relic of the past. A village nearby called Mataria stands on the site of the old city. This is a Christian place of pilgrimage because of the Tree of the Virgin where the Holy Family is said to have rested on their journey, and there is a sacred well from which they are believed to have drawn water. Close to this is the Coptic Church of the Nativity. On this side of Cairo is the new Coptic Cathedral with St Mark's tomb to which the relics of the saint were brought when they were returned to Egypt in 1968.

Hotels and Restaurants in Cairo

The following is a list of the principal hotels and a sample of some of the simpler ones used by western visitors to the Egyptian capital. Space does not permit a comprehensive list, nor is it practicable to quote prices which are liable to change from season to season. Current information on hotels and tariffs is obtainable from the offices of the Egyptian Tourist Authority in London (see General Information) and in other countries, or through travel agents.

The Nile Hilton is on the east bank close to the Tahrir Bridge from Gezira Island and adjacent to the Egyptian Museum. This is a typical Hilton, large, luxurious and providing all the facilities of a deluxe international hotel. There is also the similar Ramesses Hilton on the east bank, a few hundred metres downstream. The Meridien Hotel is built on an islet at the northern end of Roda Island and is linked to the east bank corniche road by its own causeway: this hotel has probably the best location in the whole of Cairo, being virtually on the Nile. Eighty per cent of its clientele in winter are businessmen, so it is not essentially a package-group hotel.

Also on the eastern Corniche el Nil between Tahrir Bridge and the British Embassy is Shepheard's, the most famous and evocative name among Cairo hotels, but now only one — and not the best — among many 5-star hotels. Beside it is the new luxurious Semiramis Inter-Continental where the cooking is very good. The Cairo Sheraton on the west bank is opposite the southern end of Gezira Island. It is another, large, luxurious international hotel. Opposite it on the Gezira Island is the Gezira Sheraton, and on the eastern side of the island, in Zamalek beside the July 26th Bridge, is the excellent Marriott Hotel with very good food.

The Mena House Oberoi Hotel is beside the Pyramids out at Giza and is another of the classic old hotels of Cairo. It was built as a hunting lodge for Khedive Ismail in the mid-1800s and converted into a guest house at the time of the opening of the Suez Canal. About 1880 it was converted into an hotel, and became the famous place to stay. It was traditional to have tea on its verandah and watch the sun sinking behind the Pyramids. The whole has been redecorated and brought up to date, resulting in a well equipped luxury hotel which retains much of the old romantic atmosphere.

The Siag Pyramids Hotel is a large comfortable five-star hotel on the Saqqara Road about 15 minutes' walk from the Pyramids. Food and service are not outstanding, but it is a pleasant place to stay and many of the rooms have an evocative view of the Pyramids. In the airport area of Heliopolis are the Heliopolis Movenpick, Heliopolis Sheraton, and the Heliopolis Meridien. All these hotels are in the five-star category.

There are some twelve hotels in the four-star category and, of these the Nile Savoy Hotel in Zamalek is well placed.

The official hotel guide lists about 50 in the three-star rating. The Scheherazade Hotel on the west bank of the Nile, opposite the northern half of Gezira Island is, like Shepheard's and several other

Cairo

hotels in different grades, operated by the government-owned Egyptian Hotels Company. The rooms are modern, quite comfortable and all with private bath and telephone. Most have balconies overlooking the river. The Horus House Hotel in Zamelek has been highly recommended.

Restaurants
In Cairo these are some recommendations out of the many available: Arabesque, Kasr el Nil Street, has good food and an attractive decor (it is advisable to book in advance); Felfela, Huda Sharawi St (off Talat Harb St); Five Bells in Zamalek; Four Corners, also in Zamalek by the Marriott Hotel; Swissair Restaurant beside the Cairo Sheraton. Other good ones in all the large hotels.

In the Pyramids area, the Mena House Hotel has two restaurants: the Khan El Khalili, serving Egyptian food, and the Moghul Room with Indian cuisine. Vues des Pyramids, 8, Pyramids Road is an excellent fish restaurant.

Telephone numbers are not given as many have changed recently and others may do so. Enquire on arrival in Cairo.

Night Clubs
As far as visitors are concerned, these are mainly in the principal hotels, for example the Abu-Nawas at the Mena House Hotel, the El Hambra at the Cairo Sheraton, and the Falafel at the Ramesses Hilton.

Sport
Visitors are welcome at a number of sporting clubs in Gezira, Heliopolis and Maadi where swimming, polo, golf, tennis and squash are available. See General Information for a list. In the winter there is horse racing on the Gezira course on Saturdays and Sundays.

For the ordinary tourist who simply wants to sail on the Nile in a felucca, these graceful craft can be hired with boatmen by the hour on the El Nil Corniche. They take up to ten people and the fixed charge is moderate.

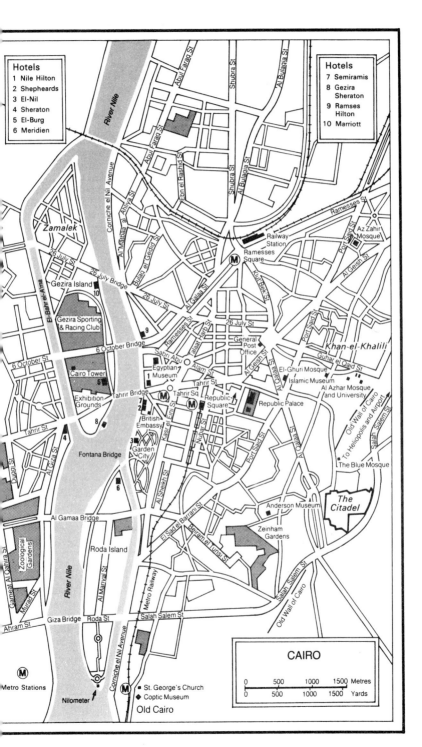

Hotels
1 Nile Hilton
2 Shepheards
3 El-Nil
4 Sheraton
5 El-Burg
6 Meridien

Hotels
7 Semiramis
8 Gezira Sheraton
9 Ramses Hilton
10 Marriott

River Nile

Abul Farag St
Shubra St
Al Bulaqia St

Zamalek

Corniche el Nil Avenue

Ebn el Rashid St

Shubra St

Al Bulaqia St

Ramesses St

Az Zahir Mosque

Railway Station
Ramesses Square

26 July St

Gezira Island

26 July Bridge

Bulaq el Gedid St

26 July St

Al Galaa St

26 July St

Gezira Sporting & Racing Club

Port Said St

Al Geish St

6 October Bridge

6 October St

Cairo Tower

Ramesses St

Sabri Abu Alam St

Talaat Harb St

General Post Office

Khan-el-Khalili

Guhar el Qaid St

Exhibition Grounds

Tahrir Bridge

Egyptian Museum

Tahrir Sq

Al Geish St

El-Ghuri Mosque
Islamic Museum

Tahrir St

British Embassy

Kasr el Eini St

Republic Square

Republic Palace

Al Azhar Mosque and University

Old Wall of Cairo

Nubar St

El-Bahr el-A'ma

Al Giza St

Garden City

Port Said St

To Heliopolis and Airport

Duqqi St

Fontana Bridge

Al Shekh St

Al Qalaa St

The Blue Mosque

Salah Salem St

Al Gamaa Bridge

El Sad el Barani St

Beram el Tunsi St

Anderson Museum

Zeinham Gardens

The Citadel

Zoological Gardens

Gameal Al Qahira St

Murad St

Roda Island

Al Manyial St

Metro Railway

Salah Salem St

Old Wall of Cairo

Giza Bridge
Roda St

Ahram St

Corniche el Nil Avenue

(M)
Metro Stations

Nilometer

CAIRO

| 0 | 500 | 1000 | 1500 Metres |
| 0 | 500 | 1000 | 1500 Yards |

■ St. George's Church
♦ Coptic Museum

Old Cairo

Step Pyramid, Saqqara

The Surroundings of Cairo

At the most basic level it is the Pyramids and the Sphinx that bring visitors to Egypt. Not in isolation of course, but because they symbolise what other peoples through the ages have known about ancient Egypt. They embody the qualities of size, age and mystery.

The Pyramids and Sphinx of Giza

As such it is hardly surprising if a first sight of them is disappointing. Not everyone finds this, but to me the three stone outlines and the man-faced lion right on the edge of the modern city were an anti-climax.

I think the reason that they are less overwhelming than expected is their perfect symmetry. One expects great height, like a mountain, and they are in fact enormous. The Great Pyramid built for Cheops is 137 metres (450 feet) high, it covers an area of 13 acres and is built of about two and a half million stone blocks each weighing about two and a half tons. Some of the blocks inside the Pyramid weigh as much as 50 tons. Yet when you see this at a distance the width of the base is so great, 225 metres (746 feet) that the height is somehow dwarfed. See them far away, as for example from the road when returning from El Fayoum or Saqqara, and these neat triangular shapes will appear suddenly, looking quite small, through the heat haze. It is only when compared with other bodies, men, women and camels, that one sees the Pyramids in proportion.

There are other reasons why this may be a disillusioning experience. A short drive of about 15 kilometres (9 miles) from Cairo by bus or taxi brings the tourists in their hundreds of thousands. The Pyramids form the easiest of all expeditions and the one virtually no visitor misses. This does not mean the trip is necessarily quick: traffic is so heavy these days that I have known the drive to take an hour. However access has been improved enormously in the past few years, and the Pyramids Road is now a three-lane dual carriageway for the whole distance. On arrival there is the flotsam and jetsam which accumulates round mass tourist attractions or pilgrimage centres: postcard and bead sellers, beggars, sweetmeat vendors, camel men vying with each other to hire you their gentle-eyed but rather alarming beasts for a ride or a photograph. Or you can hire a horse if you prefer it. Try to get the charge for a ride down to LE 7. Through much of the day the Pyramids area is a crowded noisy place, though now the vendors are much less troublesome than in the past. One has to learn the detachment that can put away the present tumult, to take you back well over 4,000 years.

There are three pyramids amongst the nine at Giza which history and visitor alike will greet by name — those of Cheops, Chephren (the son of Cheops) and Mycerinus (the son of Chephren), and they were all built during the Old Kingdom's 4th Dynasty between about 2600 and 2500 BC, but they are not unique. There is the earlier step pyramid at Saqqara and others continued to be built as pharaonic tombs for about 1,000 years. There were more than 70 of them, such as the Pyramid of Hawara which one sees at El Fayoum.

Sphinx

The Sphinx too is not the only one of its kind; there is a whole avenue of sphinxes leading to the temples of Karnak at Luxor. This one, whose face is believed to be a likeness of Chephren, is simply the most outstanding and famous. Carved from solid rock, it is 20 metres (66 feet) high and the full length of the lion's body is 72 metres (240 feet). It faces east to the rising sun. Much anxiety is felt about the preservation of the Sphinx. Restoration work carried out in the mid 1980s proved to be faulty. In 1988 a 660 lb block of stone fell from one shoulder. Egyptian and international archaeologists are now preparing a plan for restoration which will not use cement.

So — accept the crowds and the living bustle which surrounds this place. The famous dead are still masters here, and if you stay at one of the hotels nearby there will be moments when you see the Pyramids in all the evocative glory of sunset or in the night, when their great dark shapes seem even more tremendous in contrast to the modern garland of street lights below. The ancients hailed them as one of the seven wonders of the world, and the wonder endures.

Great Pyramid

Most of us will have to join a panting and perspiring line of visitors who climb up and down the duckboard ladders inside the Great Pyramid — that of Cheops — to reach the empty chamber which was built for the kingly dead. And yet, despite the crowds, one is overwhelmed by this extraordinary building, 4,500 years old, which has amazed architects and mathematicians as well as archaeologists. There are two chambers built inside the solid structure and one cut from the rock below. All are connected by passages to a single corridor which runs from the pyramid's only entrance in the north face, 17 metres (55 feet) above ground level.

Experts believe that each of the chambers was intended for the king's tomb, so that the construction embraces several changes of plan. The Grand Gallery, more than 46 metres (150 feet) long and nearly nine metres (30 feet) high leads from the ascending entrance passage to the King's chamber and that room, 10 metres (34 feet) long, five metres (17 feet) wide and six metres (19 feet) high, was guarded by three granite portcullises. Every precaution seems to have been taken to ensure that Cheops should rest undisturbed, yet only an empty sarcophagus remains.

Although from a short distance away the Pyramids appear smooth, the outer surfaces are now rough because the polished limestone blocks with which the original builders faced the exterior were plundered long ago and used for buildings in Cairo.

Round the three giants and the inscrutable Sphinx is a world of satellite pyramids and the tombs called mastabas because their shape is like a table or bench. To the west there are the tombs of nobles, courtiers and officials; to the east are those of the princesses. Pavements lead down to the pharaohs' funerary temples in a valley below. There are also pits made for barges or galleys beside the Pyramid of Cheops. One of these great wooden boats, the Royal Ship of Cheops, discovered in 1954, is about 46 metres (150 feet) long. It is now on display in a specially constructed museum just to the south of the Great Pyramid. They are thought to be connected with the solar vessel of Ra the sun god and the funerary boats by which departed souls journeyed to judgement in the underworld.

There is a museum at the foot of Cheops' Pyramid and from its garden there is a fine view of the Nile and Cairo.

Son et Lumière

A second expedition should be made to the Pyramids (unless you are staying there) to see the Son et Lumière performance. In recent years this has come to be one of the tourist highlights of a stay in Cairo, and rightly so. There are three such entertainments in Egypt, the others are the more extensive and even more evocative Karnak Son et Lumière at Luxor and one at Aswan. None should be missed. The magic and majesty of Egypt's past is on a huge scale. It does not suffer by having recorded sound, and the surrounding darkness and the changing forms of light enhance the mystery.

This one is given in front of the Sphinx. The script has been well constructed and the English version is magnificently spoken by fine actors. The audience sit in tiered seats and tickets for the performance are obtainable through travel agents. Unless staying out at Giza the simplest plan is to book for one of the inclusive packages with coach transport from the city.

Performances are given in Arabic, English, French, Italian, Spanish and German, so it is important to book for the right one. Enquire in Cairo as to which days the different languages are given, times and charges. Gramophone records of the sound track can be bought and make one of the more interesting souvenirs of an Egyptian holiday. Again, make sure you select the language you want.

There are one or two things to remember about attending the Pyramids Son et Lumière. This is an occasion when you will put to the test the warning that the desert can become cold after sundown. Even for the hour or so of this performance one can get thoroughly chilled, and it is important to take all the warm clothes you can muster for sitting out-of-doors by the Pyramids in winter. In spring and summer it is quite different and one habitually dines at the open-air restaurants here wearing light clothes, but even then a wrap or cardigan may be welcome. Secondly, mosquitoes. The Pyramids district is a particularly trying one from this point of view. If you are a bad mosquito subject, go there well provided and anointed with insect repellent, and also with some preparation for treating bites when the repellent fails you. There is a special delight in relaxing in a hotel garden or eating at one of the open air restaurants here, but insects are an inescapable hazard. In the dark at the Son et Lumière performances one is a sitting target. The Mena House Hotel is the luxury one here (see 'hotels' in the Cairo chapter) and there are others in all grades.

Memphis and Saqqara

Some whole day sightseeing tours from Cairo combine the Pyramids with Memphis and Saqqara which lie farther south, about 32 kilometres (18 miles) from the capital. With luck, one can drive there in

The Surroundings of Cairo

an hour from the city centre, but the road passes by the Pyramids and if that part of the route is crowded there will be delays. Beyond Giza, the road is narrow in parts and can also be congested, but it is a picturesque route which makes the trip enjoyable. Unless you are very short of time I suggest a separate half-day for this excursion: there is a limit to the amount of ancient history and immemorial monuments that can be assimilated and appreciated at one time.

At the beginning of the Saqqara Road, a few hundred yards from the turning off the Pyramids Road and before you reach the Siag Hotel there are several shops selling papyrus pictures. Misr National Papyrus (tel. 867890) is a good one, offering wide choice.

The road lies for part of the way along a canal and the country is green and full of life. There are numerous date palms, villages of mud brick houses and a placid, rural life moving at the tempo of sun and season rather than the arbitrary dictates of time machines. Older women in the villages of most parts of Egypt are still faithful to the traditional black garb: black galebeah with a black flowing scarf over the head. Faces are not veiled and young women and children are dressed in brilliant colours. Men wear white, light blue or green galebeahs, sometimes brown or grey, and a small white cap, often covered with a turban. In large towns the clothing of both men and women is largely European, but in the country the traditional loose flowing garments are cooler in the hot sunshine and warmer in the chill of evening.

Bullock raising water from a well. Hutchison Library

In the villages women walk sedately, carrying their goods on their heads, or standing in groups talking while the children play with an obvious delight in the basic elements of earth and water. Everywhere there are goats and the patient, all-purpose donkeys, but in these particular villages one sees few camels. Along one canal-side path I watched a man riding a mule followed by what was no doubt his complement of livestock: a cow, a donkey and a foal.

Memphis

Memphis was founded in the time of the 1st Dynasty some 5,000 years ago. Menes, the first pharaoh of this Dynasty was the unifier of the two former kingdoms, White and Red, Upper and Lower Egypt, and he chose for his capital this fertile spot below the plateau of Saqqara. It was strategically placed, just within the old territory of Lower Egypt and above the head of the Delta: commanding the vital valley region of the south and the rich fertility lying northwards. Memphis is on the west side of the Nile, Heliopolis farther down to the east.

In Memphis, Menes had a notable 'white-walled palace' and it remained the capital throughout the period of the Old Kingdom and later, until Thebes came to importance. Even in the Middle Kingdom between 2000 and 1700 BC, Memphis was still of great importance and a royal residence. Herodotus, writing 1,500 years later, described its glories. Apart from the palace its greatest building was the temple of Ptah, the artificer god and patron of smiths.

Long afterwards, in the time of the Islamic Mameluks, the dykes built to protect the city from the waters of the Nile were breached, and the seasonal floods inundated the remains of the ancient city covering the relics of its past magnificence with alluvial mud.

Today there is very little left to us of Memphis, and what there is provides evidence of its continuance rather than its beginnings. There is a vast recumbent statue of Ramesses II, who lived in the 13th century BC some 1,700 years after the first Menes founded Memphis, enclosed in a modern protective building and, outside, a remarkable sphinx carved from one block of alabaster with the face of the same pharaoh. A little distance away some of the ruins of the great Temple of Ptah have been excavated, but this too was rebuilt in the Ramesside period, and again by Ramesses II. There was no reverence for antiquity then.

Cities of the living are continually changing and developing. Cities of the dead have no present; they are always commemorating the past and awaiting the future. Today in our time-conscious west even the dead are sometimes only allowed a limited number of years to occupy their grave-space undisturbed, and there are of course many old cemeteries and churchyards where the ground has been re-used for burials. But generally speaking, both religious respect and pagan superstition agree in leaving burial grounds alone. That and the fact that they were usually built of enduring substances is why so much of what we know about the past in many parts of the world is derived from barrows, tombs, mausoleums and gravestones, although they were so often robbed of all valuables.

The ancient Egyptians as we know were much concerned with death and the after life, and so great care and time was spent during a pharaoh's lifetime in preparing a tomb worthy to receive him. Space was important too, and thus there were these great separate areas well away from the living towns. Luxor's city of the dead is across the river from the site of ancient Thebes. Memphis' pharaonic burial ground is a little distance away at Saqqara, and there much more remains than of Memphis proper.

Saqqara
Chief among its treasures is the Step Pyramid, which is one of the most important buildings in Egypt because it is not only the first pyramid but also the earliest massive stone-built structure known to history. It was erected as the tomb of Zoser, pharaoh of the 3rd Dynasty, and the architect was Imhotep, a surgeon and administrator who was later deified and identified with the Greek god of medicine, Asklepios. History has always honoured him as one of the earliest figures in the study of science and medicine.

This pyramid is named for its form: it is built in ridges of stone — steps — rather than with the smooth surface of later pyramids in their original form. One theory is that it was designed as a ladder up to heaven. Elaborate precautions were taken when Zoser was entombed: his remains were enclosed in a granite-lined chamber at the bottom of a deep pit, but despite this the place was penetrated and rifled in very ancient times. One leg bone of the king was found by the British excavator Howard-Wyse when he was digging under the pyramid in the mid-19th century but nothing more of Zoser. Other archaeologists however found grave-goods there: 20,000 beautiful alabaster jars, some of which had probably contained food offerings.

Stone Necropolis
Imhotep built a great stone necropolis at Saqqara as well as the Pyramid, the whole being an incredible innovation as earlier buildings had all been of mud bricks. Great underground galleries have been discovered here, which were filled with votive offerings of mummified falcons, ibis birds, baboons and sacred bulls. One of the weird experiences for the visitor is to walk along a great corridor, dark and musty, between tombs of bulls some of which were added in the time of Ramesses II, all dedicated to the cult of the bull god Apis.

There are other pyramids at Saqqara, more than a dozen of them, notably those of Unas and Oserkaf, and hundreds of mastabas and tombs. The finest of these is that of Ti who was an important man at court in the late 6th Dynasty period. The wall decorations here give a vivid picture of Egyptian life at that time.

Altogether Saqqara's necropolis is a kind of funerary panorama of relics which extended from the 1st to the 30th Dynasties, a span of about 2,700 years. The earliest mummy was discovered here, and also the oldest papyrus. To me its past is more accessible and the feeling of the greatness of the kingdoms of the Nile is easier to experience here than at the Pyramids of Giza. Also there is more feeling of space, for the desert still virtually surrounds it and a minor sandstorm can drive one to shelter in the lee of the Step Pyramid with one's mouth full of grit.

There is plenty to do to make this a place of present enjoyment too. Most people will walk from one site to another, but you can hire the colourful and traditional forms of transport on the spot. If you seek experience, try the camel. To me, there is no more uncomfortable means of locomotion, or more frightening on the first occasion, when your mount rises from its knees in sections, tipping the rider backwards and forwards in the process. The expert camel rider has my most profound admiration and wonder. Camel races are marvellous things to watch, and even more marvellous to those who have ridden a few anxious yards on these rolling ships of the desert.

Refreshments and souvenirs of the more popular kind are available at Saqqara, but all these things somehow do not impinge on the mood of the place. In a way they reflect the Islamic way of enjoying a family day out in company with the dead. In Egypt as in other Moslem lands you will often find fathers, mothers and children picnicking happily on a Friday or some greater holiday among the graves of their forebears, the children playing and the elders talking and eating cheerfully in the sunshine. It is the materialism of the modern west that makes death so fearful and distasteful.

El Fayoum Oasis

A very easy excursion from Cairo, yet one which comparatively few visitors make is to El Fayoum. This is Egypt's largest oasis which lies about 100 kilometres (62 miles) south of the capital and not far from the Nile. Fayoum appears on some of the Cairo tour operators' lists as a full day trip, or it is easily visited independently with a hired car. The drive from the heart of Cairo to the town of Fayoum in the centre of the oasis takes two hours or less.

For the seeker after stark experience, Fayoum is almost too easy.

The Surroundings of Cairo

The road is good and is not overcrowded once you are past Giza and Saqqara. It is over real bare sandy desert and the transition into the rich fertility of the oasis is sudden and complete.

It is all exactly what the newcomer expects except that El Fayoum is much too large. The popular conception of an oasis is that of a group of palm trees surrounding a pool, a few mud houses and two or three camels feeding as they rest in the midst of a long journey over the immemorial caravan routes, all surrounded by barren wastes of sand. This is a large fertile region of 1,800 square kilometres, with a population of about 1¼ million and its own administrative governorate. As such it hardly seems an oasis to the foreigner because once you are in it you forget the desert, but it is an attractive and interesting area, among the most productive in the country and very well worth visiting.

The first impression is green and clean. There are thousands of date palms and feathery casuarina trees and water channels run beside the road. There are virtually no springs in El Fayoum except some mineral ones; water is brought from the Nile by the Yousef Canal and is carried through the whole area by a network of small canals, levels being raised by water wheels which have become the symbol of Fayoum. There is, however, one large natural lake in the north, Lake Qarun, the origin of the natural oasis.

Between the irrigation channels there are carefully tended fields and orchards. Oranges, mangoes, grapes, figs, bananas, guavas, olives and peanuts are all grown here. The villages of brown mud brick houses are clustered beside the water, and the life seems much more prosperous than in most other areas of Egypt except in the Delta.

Women dressed in brightly coloured galebeahs walk purposefully, carrying jars, cans or great baskets on their heads. Men are working in the fields, children play under the trees, gather at the schools or help on the land. One tiny boy drives a lumbering water buffalo across a field, thwacking it proudly on the rump with a long stick.

Fayoum Town

Almost in the centre is the town of Fayoum itself with 300,000 inhabitants: it is the commercial and market centre of the area and the best starting point from which to explore. One can lunch quite pleasantly at an open air restaurant in the square known simply and unromantically as the Cafeteria. Its terrace overlooks two of the typical great black water wheels and the gentle plash as they turn adds a cooling, soothing quality to the not very hectic sounds of the streets beyond.

The town has a number of mosques, one of which dates from 1476, when it was built by a Mameluk Sultan, Qait Bey, but the history of Fayoum goes far back into the times of the Pharaohs. It was important during the period of the Middle Kingdom, about 2000 - 1800 BC, and again in the Ptolemaic and Roman eras.

Hawara Pyramid
One long afternoon is sufficient to see most of the places of special interest. Fourteen kilometres (9 miles) south-east of the town at Hawara is the pyramid of Amenemhat III, a king of the 12th Dynasty who was buried here in about 1900 BC. At that time the pharaohs had their residence neither at Memphis nor Thebes but in a city called Lisht just to the north-east of the Fayoum oasis. This pyramid was built of mud bricks covered with a facing of limestone. Its entrance was made facing south instead of north as in earlier pyramids, which is said to have been a device to mislead thieves who might seek to rob the tomb of gold and jewels buried with the king. Whether this was successful is not clear, for the pyramid temple was apparently plundered officially by the architects of Ramesses II for their own purposes, carrying away statues and works of art to be incorporated in their own constructions.

Today the Hawara pyramid stands silent and worn among sand-hills. The tomb of Amenemhat III's daughter Nefru-Ptah was discovered some two kilometres (one mile) away in 1956. At Lahun about 12 kilometres (seven miles) farther south-east there are more pyramids and mastabas, the tombs of nobles and princesses.

Lake Qarun
Lake Qarun has shrunk with the centuries. In the great days of the Middle Kingdom when it was called Moeris it apparently covered almost half the low-lying area which is now irrigated, but even today it covers about 200 square kilometres. Then it was full of sacred crocodiles, associated with the crocodile god Sobek. The Greeks called the provincial capital here Crocodopolis, but sacred or profane they have all gone now and the lake is a great place for bird life. Duck and other migrating species from Europe and north-west Asia come in winter, and it is popular with Egyptian shooting parties and picnickers. It is also the source of fish for all local inhabitants.

Selyin
Selyin, on the road between Fayoum town and the lake, is a most surprising place. Here are the mineral springs, and gardens, bridges, paved paths and seats and a 'casino' (which here means a restaurant and not a gaming centre) have been built. It has the quiet, restful but slightly seedy appearance of many of the smaller European spas and seems totally out of keeping with deserts and oases, pharaohs or the worship of reptiles.

The Surroundings of Cairo

Kom Oshim

By far the most interesting place, to me, is Kom Oshim, on the northern edge of the Fayoum area and just beyond the eastern end of the lake, from which it is little more than an hour's drive back to Cairo. At Kom Oshim are the ruins of a Graeco-Roman town — Karanis — with the remains of two temples. The whole is a wide spreading area of sandy hummocks, broken walls and the indefinable sense of buried history; of human stories and great events to which the key may lie unguessed beneath our feet.

Karanis was first excavated by a team from Michigan University in 1935. Much later, after 1952, further work was undertaken by the University of Cairo. There are remains of two Roman baths here, built of brick while the temples were of sandstone. It must have been quite an important city. Evidence has been found in this area of efforts to irrigate a vineyard by filling depressions in the ground level left from the ancient well-watered era before Lake Moeris began to shrink. Further channels were dug to bring water from a branch of the Yousef Canal, but this particular effort does not seem to have been successful.

Beside the area of the ruined city there is now the small but admirably arranged and very interesting Kom Oshim Museum. When I last visited it I found the curator an enthusiast and very knowledgeable. He was a mine of information about the traditional ways of life in the oasis as well as its history. For example, the spinning mill at Fayoum town which has brought work to the area and uses the locally produced cotton, or the different kinds of dates, green or yellow, and how they are still wiped and stored in pottery jars as was done by the people of 5,000 years ago.

The exhibits in the museum were all discovered within the governorate, though of course not all of what was found is here; many of the most precious objects have been taken to Cairo, Alexandria or abroad. Still, here are examples of many things: mummy cases, jewellery, pottery, canopic jars in which the internal organs of the mummified body were sealed. There are pieces of huge statues and tiny, delicate rings and ornaments. One charmingly human exhibit is a little row of figures displaying different types of coiffure, the advertising aids of some enterprising hairdresser. The museum which was opened in 1974 has treasures from most of the area's different phases: Pharaonic, Greek, Roman, Coptic, Islamic and modern.

This completes the circuit of the best known sites of El Fayoum. Where time is limited and the traveller wants to explore as much of Egypt as possible he would not really be justified in lingering here when the country has so many and such varied treasures to reveal, but for anyone who is staying for some time, Fayoum deserves attention.

There are other Pharaonic monuments including the Obelisk of Ebgige, towns dating from the centuries of Greek and Roman occupation, and temples such as Om Elborigate, Kkasr Qarun and Kasr El-Sagha. There is the Coptic monastery of El-Azab and the church of St George, several interesting mosques, and the 700-year-old Lahun Barrage built by the Sultan Zahir Baibars to regulate irrigation. In addition, there are the attractions of the lake, the placid countryside, the sunshine and the water-wheels.

Local hotels
To enjoy all this at leisure one would need to stay in the area. The best known hotel, the four-star Auberge, is on Lake Qarun. There is the Panorama, classified three-star, at Shakshouk, also on the shores of the lake, and the two-star Selyin Hotel at Selyin village. Visitors should make enquiries before arriving because the Fayoum accommodation is limited.

Helwan

This is a very different excursion from the capital, much nearer, more sophisticated. Indeed Helwan, which is only about 30 kilometres (18 miles) from the centre of Cairo, is considered one of its more elegant suburbs. It lies to the south-east of the city and is therefore east of the Nile, so cannot be combined with Giza, Saqqara and Fayoum away to the west.

In the modern life of the country Helwan is a popular spa reached by road along the Nile Corniche or by train or metro. There is also a regular bus service from Ramesses Square. The town stands on a plateau and has a good winter climate. Six hot sulphur springs are the source of its thermal treatments for osteo-arthritis, rheumatoid arthritis and various nerve and respiratory conditions and skin diseases, but these are not really geared for European patients.

Near the Helwan metro terminus there are extensive and colourful souks selling fruit, vegetables, clothing, hardware, everything in fact except tourist junk! This is the town's real local market centre, and well worth exploring.

For the holiday visitor the chief places of interest are the Observatory, the Japanese Garden, Cabritage Casino and the Wax Museum. Study of the stars and astrology were sciences of the ancient Egyptians and have continued through the ages. The Helwan Observatory was built in 1903, the site being chosen because of its excellent weather conditions. It is open to visitors on Wednesday afternoons, but it would be advisable to check on this in case of changes in the opening times.

The Japanese Garden claims to be the only one of its kind in the

Middle East, and even to the visitor who comes to Egypt to see and experience things Egyptian, there may be a certain piquancy in seeing it, though at present it appears to be rather neglected.

Cabritage Casino is not a gambling establishment but a simple kind of leisure and refreshment centre with large gardens and a swimming pool.

Limestone is quarried at Tura and Ma'sara close to Helwan today as it was in Pharaonic days, and for those who are interested there are some fascinating old drawings at the quarries showing the early methods of stone working.

The Wax Museum, no doubt inspired by Madame Tussaud, was opened in Cairo nearly 50 years ago and moved to Helwan in 1955. It contains wax effigies and scenes of famous characters and events in the history of Egypt. Here you will find tableaux of Akhenaton and Queen Nefertiti with their family and royal entourage journeying to the Aton Temple at Tel-el-Amarna; Pharaoh's daughter with the infant Moses rescued from the rushes; Salah-el-Din visiting his sick enemy, England's Richard Coeur de Lion; Caliph Umar Ibn el-Khattab visiting a humble family, and a typical wedding of the last century. NOTE: The Wax Museum is not in the centre of the town, but at Ain Helwan, one station nearer Cairo on the metro line.

The Nile Barrages

Near the head of the Delta and some 25 kilometres (16 miles) north west of Cairo the great river divides into two, the Damietta branch entering the Mediterranean just west of Port Said and that of Rosetta a little east of Alexandria. The Barrages are at the point of division and this is a popular park-like area where local people go for picnics. The original barrage was built about 100 years ago by Mohamed Ali and was the first major engineering operation to control the flow of the Nile. The second one was built in the early 20th century.

Half-day package tours by car are available from Cairo by which you are driven through the old and new barrages, visit the Hydraulic Museum and the charming Botanic Gardens.

The Monasteries of Wadi Natrun

The valley of Wadi Natrun can be visited as a long day's excursion from either Cairo or Alexandria. It is about halfway between the two and some two hours' drive from either via the Desert Road. Or if you are travelling from one city to the other by car it can be visited en route.

This is a visit for those particularly interested in the Coptic Church and its fundamental and current life in the history of Egypt. It is said that there were once 500 Coptic monasteries in the Western Desert and some 50,000 monks. The Coptic call of monasticism was always to the desert. Many of the monks lived semi-hermit lives in solitary cells or caves, meeting only for a weekly mass and a communal meal or 'agape'. The tradition continued through the centuries, surviving the Islamic zeal of Arab invaders in the 7th century and later persecutions. Theirs was a very simple, austere life inspired by saintly men who taught and prayed and meditated.

Three of the most famous of the surviving monasteries are in this single valley. These are Deir Amba Bishoi, Deir es-Suryani and Deir Macarius.

At Deir Amba Bishoi there is a holy tree, a very ancient tamarisk known as the Tree of Ephraim, which is specially venerated by the monks and now protected by a surrounding wall. Close by is a well dating from Roman times where it is believed that the swords were washed which had slain 40 Christian martyrs.

Deir es-Suryani is a creamy-grey complex of buildings about five kilometres (three miles) from the main road and enclosed in walls more than nine metres (30 feet) high. There is a modern belfry, a square keep-like building, chapels and other monastic buildings. There is a deep sense of unchanging faith and tradition: monks chant as they stand beneath worn and sometimes peeling frescoes. One of the basic vows — poverty — is patently observed, and the faith shines all the stronger for the simplicity of those who live and die here.

These monasteries still seem to live in an unchanging timelessness, but, Deir Macarius, has moved into our own times to meet the needs of a new increase in monastic vocations. It was founded by Father Macarius the Great in about AD 350, destroyed, rebuilt in the 9th and 11th centuries, and no doubt continued like the others until the Coptic renewal called for a place for many new entrants from different walks of life. Much of the beauty and dignity of the past has been sacrificed to the functional needs of an order which is as essentially practical as the Christian faith itself.

Prior application for a visit to these monasteries in not now necessary (see General Information).

Karnak Temple, Luxor

Up the Nile:
Cairo to Luxor

Above Cairo, that is southwards, the Nile becomes more and more the spinal cord which co-ordinates the life and movement of the country. Thus it has always been, and so it remains today, for though circumstances may change the vital elements do not.

The river with its natural floods and man-made dams and irrigation systems controls the habitable and cultivable area of land and is the life blood of new projects, such as those associated with the vast Nasser Lake. It has always been a highway, for the prevailing northerly winds carried sailing boats upstream and the current down, and today other routes such as road and rail follow the valley.

In Lower Egypt the Nile itself divides for its progress through the Delta. Life, industry and development are diversified and mixed with the influences of the Mediterranean, the Suez Canal and the Red Sea. The flow of foreign people through Cairo and this area is constant for it is, in the modern world, at the focal point of Africa and the Middle East. This is where the Egyptian population explosion is going on and where the great developments and the great problems exist.

Upper Egypt is still a different world, yet it starts only some 50 kilometres (31 miles) south of Cairo. Of course the transition is gradual, but it begins once you are clear of the capital, partly no doubt because of the geographical situation. The Red Sea is well over 100 kilometres (62 miles) to the east across arid and often mountainous desert: to the west lie the much greater expanses of the Sahara. Life and movement is inevitably channelled into this north-south axis.

Therefore we shall follow this natural course which takes us deeper into the world of ancient Egypt. Not farther back in actual time — the Pyramids of Giza are earlier landmarks than anything one sees farther south — but into a world where the past still possesses great powers for various reasons, many of them unashamedly economic.

At different times in history the centre of importance in the Nile valley has changed. When Lower and Upper Egypt were united in 3000 BC, it was naturally at a focal point between the two that Memphis was established as the capital. Later the focus moved much farther south to Thebes and remained there, reaching a peak in the 18th and 19th Dynasties, until the Assyrian invasion in 700 BC. Later still with the Greeks and Romans it centred round the Mediterranean port at Alexandria and the Cairo area. Today the focus is Cairo. But for the visitor whose deepest interest is always likely to remain rooted in the most famous era of ancient Egypt the focal point is still Thebes, which today is called Luxor.

Comparatively few short term visitors will make the whole trip from Cairo to Aswan by river, though there are a few leisurely cruises available for the complete journey. Between Luxor and Aswan there is an ever growing number of ships, and we shall follow that reach specifically from the cruise angle. Usually the long stretch of almost 700 kilometres (434 miles) up to Luxor will be covered by road or by train, halting at various points en route. Many people will omit this section altogether, travelling by air or rail direct to Luxor.

El Minya to Abydos

Assuming then that one makes this journey by road, the first place of importance to the visitor is El Minya on the west bank, the centre of its own governorate and some 250 kilometres (155 miles) south of Cairo. It has the four-star ETAP Nefertit Minya Hotel, two in the two-star category, Lotus and El Shatee, and the one-star Ibn Khassib.

From here there are several places of historic interest to visit by car or taxi. Beni Hassan is on the opposite bank and about 20 kilometres (12 miles) south; a visit involves a steamer trip from El

Up the Nile: Cairo to Luxor

Minya or a drive along the west bank to Abu Gurgas and then a river crossing by boat. Beni Hassan has some 39 tombs going back to the Middle Kingdom (2060-1789 BC) and several of the most important have remarkably vivid wall pictures: scenes of everyday life of those times — sports, dancing, hunting, children at play, battles, bird life.

Al Ashmunein is reached from Mallawi, to the south of Beni Hassan, but on the same side of the Nile as El Minya. Al Ashmunein was called 'Hermopolis the Great' by the Greeks, but has relics of temples going back to the 18th Dynasty, the beginning of the Ramesside period, and others continuing right through to the Christian era. It was particularly important under the Greeks. Some of the discoveries made here are now in the museum at Mallawi.

Tel el-Amarna is on the east bank about 10 kilometres (6 miles) from the river and is reached by crossing the Nile by boat at Deir Mawas and thence by tractor or donkey. Historically this place is especially interesting because it was the city created by Akhenaton when he established his monotheist religion, the worship of the one god and father whom he called Aton. Leaving Thebes, so long dedicated to the cult of Amun, Akhenaton built his new capital city here. The most important remains are Akhenaton's tomb and that of his beautiful wife Nefertiti, and also some other members of the royal family. The fame of Amarna like the fervency of the King's faith really died with Akhenaton, and Tutankhamun soon restored the old religion at Thebes.

The next town of any importance up the river is Asyut. It is rooted in ancient times, and is a centre of Christianity in Upper Egypt. The name means sentinel or watchman, no doubt because it stood at a vantage point on the Nile.

Next comes Suhag which, like Asyut is on the west bank of the Nile and is within about 150 kilometres (93 miles) of Luxor.

Abydos

Just west from Suhag, about 12 kilometres (7½ miles) from the Nile, is Abydos. Here we are as near the beginning of things in Egypt as one can be. On this site was the city of This or Thinis which is believed to have been one of the earliest human settlements in the Nile Valley. Before the foundation of Memphis, pharoahs of the united Upper and Lower Kingdoms coming from Upper Egypt were buried at Abydos and not in their new territories to the north. The cult of Osiris was strong here, for Osiris' tomb was believed to be in this area and it was a great centre of pilgrimage for the ancients.

But there is nothing to see from the very early times. Abydos' chief monument is the Temple of Seti I (19th Dynasty) which replaced an earlier building and was itself enlarged and completed by Seti's son Ramesses II. It is dedicated to Osiris and some Egyptologists consider it the finest of all Egypt's surviving temples as it dates from the peak period of pharaonic art. If you can come to Abydos, allow plenty of time for the visit. The wall pictures and reliefs are very fine and it was from a series of 70 cartouches here, together with other sources, that experts were able to work out the definite order and date pattern of the dynasties.

It is a pity that Abydos is so difficult to reach unless you are driving the whole way up the Nile Valley. Comparatively few visitors come here, though cars can be hired from Luxor, the trip taking about three hours each way. There are also a few trains from Asyut to Sohag, from where there is local transport to the site (12 kilometres). Those Nile cruises which come all the way up from Cairo stop at Nag Hamadi a little farther south, from which excursions to Abydos are organised.

Dendara and Qena

Above this the Nile makes a wide bend to the east and at its centre is the town of Qena where there is another very famous temple at Dendara. This is a later temple, built on an ancient site by Ptolemy III and not completed until the Roman period. Dedicated to Hathor, goddess of love and joy, who was the patron deity of Dendara, it is an example of what earnest devotees of pure Egyptian art and architecture consider decadent: the old classic styles are mixed with Greek and Roman influence. The paintings of the sky and the zodiac are famous: there are secret chambers too, set deep in the thickness of the walls and foundations, and once used for stores. They were closed with huge movable stone slabs disguised by pictures which formed a part of the adjacent wall decoration.

The temple is surrounded by a wall of unfired bricks and within the enclosed area there are two houses provided for the birth of Hathor's children. One dates from the 30th Dynasty, the last of the pharaonic regimes, and the second is Roman. There is also a temple of Isis, a sacred lake and a Coptic church.

Dendara, which is most easily visited on a day trip from Luxor, is on the west side of the Nile, while Qena town is on the east, but there is a bridge over the river here. Qena is a sizable place, capital of its governorate and a market and small industrial centre for the area. It has the three-star Aluminium Hotel, and one-star New Palace, but few visitors are likely to wish to stay here as it is only another 65 kilometres (40 miles) to Luxor. It is also the starting point for two roads right across the Eastern Desert to the Red Sea, one to Safaga and the other to Hurghada, about three hours' drive in each case. They start as one road from Qena.

Up the Nile: Cairo to Luxor

From Qena to Luxor the road passes through rich green fertile country along the eastern bank of the river. It is a bumpy but picturesque road and an absorbing hour's drive. The countryside is not so very different from the well watered villages near Saqqara or in El Fayoum, but here we are further south and the climate is hotter and drier apart from the life-giving flow of the Nile.

Because of this, the roadside villages are gathered under thick clusters of palm trees while the people move sedately about their life and work. So do the animals, donkeys and the occasional camel: even the goats, eager and capable of finding nourishment in the most unlikely places do not seem to hurry. Only the children run sometimes, or stand watching with bright brown eyes, the girls with thick dark curls, their brothers with neatly barbered heads. Boys are boys in Egypt; you will never confuse the sexes through clothing or hairstyle except perhaps among some very modern students in Cairo. All around one sees a quiet, hard-working, rural world, blessed by an easy climate but part of a still under-developed country struggling to bring a rapidly growing population into the modern world. There is little to be seen of modernity here except the road itself. How strange that thousands of years ago this was close to the very hub of a great civilisation.

Probably the peasants did not live so very differently then. Houses made of sun-dried mud, simple graceful clothing, fishermen with their boats and nets, donkeys and bullocks. But not very far away there was a different culture: with kings revered as gods, priests and scientists, dancers and sumptuous feasts, musicians and warriors. There were treasuries of vast wealth and architects devising temples of stupendous size.

Luxor

This is a place which greets her visitors with a gentle charm, and to be frank that is surprising: it is not a quality which normally springs to mind in relation to places connected with the great heritage of Egypt's past, nor its historic figures. Did Nefertiti possess charm as well as beauty? Was it charm that made Nefertari Ramesses II's favourite wife? We do not know. Cleopatra yes, but then she came in the later, decadent, Ptolemaic times. Power, splendour, awe, beauty these were inherent in the creation of the great cities of ancient Egypt and their combined spirit lingers in the broken temples and palaces that remain. But charm makes the desolation and wonder comfortable for lesser mortals.

Luxor has a special quality: it belongs to the past, in fact to two pasts — to the great, magnificent era of Thebes which lasted for 1,000 years, and to the past of the British who came here, with many other Europeans, in the second half of the 19th century and the first third of this one. Although there are many new hotels and certain other innovations, the mood of Luxor has not moved forward very much since the 1930s. That is why it is so delightful, so endearing and sometimes so amusing.

Luxor Town

Luxor stands on the east bank of the Nile, with a long corniche road like a promenade bordering the river. This is where the cruise ships moor, and steps lead down to paths and jetties just above water level. There are green banks and trees and brightly coloured flowers; roses, oleanders and bougainvillea.

Along the corniche are the principal hotels of which some details are given later, the evocative ruins of Luxor Temple, the new Visitors' Centre and, towards the northern, Karnak, end of the river frontage, the Museum. Behind is a network of streets where there are souks, mosques, and Coptic churches.

All this is best explored on foot, with due regard to horse carriages, cars and bicycles. Traffic is not very heavy, but at dusk or after dark it is important to remember that their lights are not always wholly efficient and many bicycles have no lights at all and may be ridden on the wrong side of the road — on the left.

Transport

The air is filled with the powerful odour of horse, for the fiacre type of horse-drawn carriage, known as a calèche, is still the traditional means of transport for visitors. These carriages take two people comfortably, sitting under the hood which can be raised or folded down according to heat and taste; two others can sit rather more precariously on the small seat opposite, with their backs to the driver. That should be the limit, for the sake of the single, often emaciated horse, and for safety, but festive Egyptian parties will sometimes pack in many more children.

It is interesting that where horse carriages have been retained or reintroduced in some European cities such as Vienna they are in themselves a tourist attraction and priced accordingly. In Egypt a carriage remains cheaper than a taxi.

There are plenty of them in Luxor and the drivers vie with each other for custom, waiting in rows at the top of the steps from the cruise ship moorings, outside hotels, in the square and especially outside the entrance to the Karnak temples. There are official rates (known by English speaking guides as a 'fix-ed price') from the ships to Karnak — about three kilometres (two miles) — and back. Ask the current price before you leave the ship. A one-way drive into the town should be about LE 2, though drivers will usually ask more, and it is advisable to bargain beforehand if you want to keep the carriage for an hour or so to drive around Luxor. Never pay until the end. The driver will tell you his number and it is important to remember this and to try to memorise the appearance of both carriage and driver, though the latter are expert at finding their own passengers. Lists of 'fix-ed prices' are in fact displayed on a metal plate on each calèche, in the tourist office and elsewhere. This form of transport is picturesque, but the constant soliciting for business by calèche drivers as they pass you is becoming a major irritation of Luxor.

Members of organised groups will find that carriage transport is arranged and paid for by tour managers or guides as far as the principal expeditions are concerned.

Sightseeing
The visitor who comes to Luxor on a package holiday will of course have only a certain allocation of time, which will certainly include the principal sights and probably an hour or two to indulge in shopping. If you come independently, try to give more time to Luxor. It is a leisurely place. Its historic highlights are obvious but will repay endless return visits if your interest goes deeper.

Luxor is not like Cairo or Alexandria or Suez. It subsists on tourism; traditionally its trade and prosperity stem from the visitor, but this trade is already so old that it has a fascination of its own.

There are a few traditional dragomen in flowing galebeah and spotless white turbans, tall and probably rather portly, escorting their honoured clients in a manner which combines that of a steward and a father. Then there are the sellers of beads and imitation scarabs, sweetmeats and postcards. The sun beats down on them intensely in summer, more gently at other times, while a soft wind blows their long robes and stirs the dust about their feet.

It must have been the same when Victorian visitors came here, and though Thomas Cook now has a fine new office outside the New Winter Palace Hotel, the representatives would have provided equally reliable information at the turn of the century as that available now. But in those days the trade would have been more seasonal. Today visitors flock to Egypt all the year round, but in the past Europeans avoided the hottest months unless they had to work in the country. Egypt and especially Luxor was considered a winter haven.

There are three great 'sights' at Luxor. The smallest, but no less interesting than the others is the site of Luxor Temple round which the present town stands. The second is the great temple area of Karnak on the same east side of the Nile and just at the edge of the town to the north. The third is on the opposite side of the river and includes the Valleys of the Kings and Queens and various mortuary temples. This area of tombs is often known as Thebes of the Dead.

Most people go round these places, in large guided groups. It really is advisable to have a guide for the first visit anyway, to point out and explain the ground plan and the importance of certain places. Without personal explanation you can miss much. On the other hand, as one of a herd moving among more herds where the guides' voices create little pools of concentration in different languages, you also miss much: especially the power of silence.

The ideal would be to return alone after hiring a personal guide for the first visit. The tourist office can direct you to an agency such as Misr Travel who can supply guides. Or go round once with a guided tour and then return alone. If you have time in Luxor you can do this easily, except for the west bank city of the dead where you need transport to get from one area to another, and that can be expensive. In the case of Luxor temple and Karnak you can even wait outside till the large groups have finished their tour, then pay your entrance fee and enjoy relative solitude.

The Temple of Luxor
Right at the heart of the present town and beside the river the area of these ruins has been a place of worship for about 3,400 years. The name Luxor, by the way, has no ancient significance: it is derived from the Arabic El Uqsur which means 'the castles' and probably referred to these temple ruins as they were seen after the Arabs came to Egypt. The town's earliest name was Nût. The Greeks always knew it as Thebes which is the usual name still for the ancient city, but as that embraced the other and larger temple complex of Karnak this particular temple is known as that of Luxor.

It was built by Amenhotep III of the 18th Dynasty in the 15th century BC, and it was dedicated to the trinity of gods Amun-Re, his wife Mut and their son Khonsu. Later the ubiquitous Ramesses II (19th Dynasty) enlarged it, building a great court and adding a number of statues of himself and two obelisks. It is one of these which is now in the Place de la Concorde in Paris, having been given by Mohamed Ali to Louis Philippe in 1831, at a time when much of the temple was covered by rubble and humble Egyptian dwellings.

Today one enters through the great court of Ramesses II for a charge of LE 3. These courts were where the common people gathered for the great festivals and times of worship, the pharoah, priests and entourage going into the actual roofed temple beyond. The roofs became progressively lower towards the centre, the holy of holies, so that the sound of chanting and music was magnified as through a megaphone to the waiting crowds outside.

Now these roofs are gone and one wanders among the great columns, through courts and colonnades with striking reliefs and some wall paintings still glowing with bright colours; grass and sometimes wild flowers among the fallen stones.

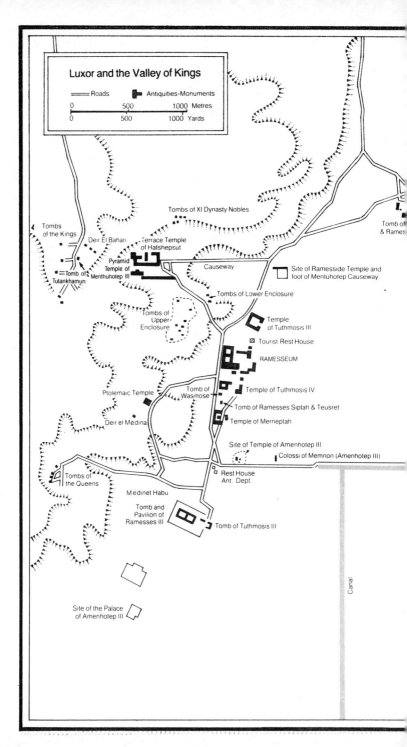

Luxor and the Valley of Kings

Roads   Antiquities-Monuments

| 0 | 500 | 1000 Metres |

| 0 | 500 | 1000 Yards |

Tombs of XI Dynasty Nobles

Tombs
of the Kings

Deir El Bahari

Terrace Temple
of Hatshepsut

Pyramid
Temple of
Menthuhotep III

Tomb of
Tutankhamun

Causeway

Tomb of
& Rames

Site of Ramesside Temple and
foot of Mentuhotep Causeway

Tombs of Lower Enclosure

Tombs of
Upper
Enclosure

Temple
of Tuthmosis III

Tourist Rest House

RAMESSEUM

Ptolemaic Temple

Tomb of
Wasmose

Temple of Tuthmosis IV

Tomb of Ramesses Siptah & Teusret

Deir el Medina

Temple of Merneptah

Site of Temple of Amenhotep III

Colossi of Memnon (Amenhotep III)

Tombs of
the Queens

Rest House
Ant. Dept.

Medinet Habu

Tomb and
Pavilion of
Ramesses III

Tomb of Tuthmosis III

Site of the Palace
of Amenhotep III

Canal

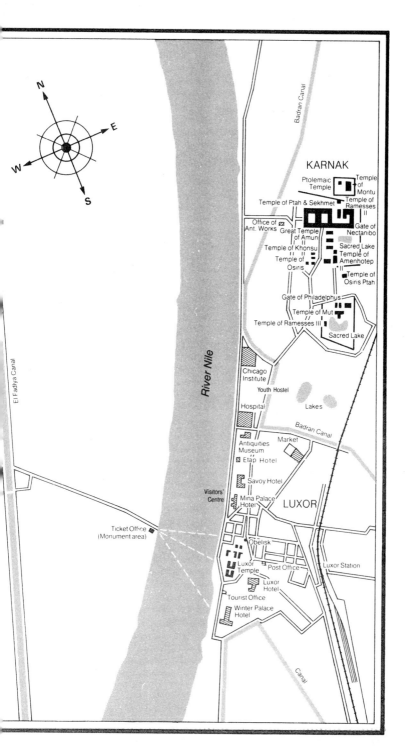

Up the Nile: Cairo to Luxor

In the Christian era a church was made at the heart of the pagan temple. The Emperor Constantine recorded his visit on a Christian altar here and the tourist will be shown the ruined church within the ruined temple. The guide may talk about the enormities of early Christians who defaced the ancient beauties of carvings. Moslems did the same of course, in various places, and the pharaonic architects were no preservationists. Ramesses II spent his 67 years' reign making everything bigger and more imposing but not necessarily better. Each century made changes, which is why an Egyptologist will urge you to take the earliest part of this temple, that built for Amenhotep II, as the true and best temple style of the New Kingdom.

In the court of Ramesses III high up on the left hand side is a manifestation of the later faith of Islam — blue tiles and a door suspended as it were high above our heads — the mosque of Abu El-Haggag. This is particularly interesting for two reasons: it shows the depth to which the temple area was buried by the accumulation of sand and debris through the centuries, and it maintains the tradition of active worship today.

The door we see up there once opened at ground level, and the small mosque behind it is still reached by a relatively short flight of steps from the town square on the farther side. I have visited it from there; a simple, peaceful place with worn carpets and a gravely courteous doorkeeper.

Luxor Museum
Apart from Luxor Temple, the Museum is the chief place of historical interest when exploring on foot and at leisure. The collection of antiquities is beautifully arranged and housed in a modern building towards the northern end of the corniche. Half an hour will suffice to see all the exhibits: statues of pharaohs, inscriptions, jewellery, treasures and relics of many kinds found in the ruins of Thebes. There is also some Coptic work.

I was haunted by the sad, thoughtful face of Sesostris III, a pharaoh of the 12th Dynasty during the Middle Kingdom around 1850 BC. This is a head carved in red granite and found at Karnak. Unlike so many formal representations this must be a genuine likeness.

The museum is only open in the evenings: 1700-2200 in summer, 1600-2100 in winter. Charge LE 3.

Shopping
Sooner or later, and for many people sooner, there will be the urge for shopping and Luxor is as good a place as any for this. Lying back from the river in the network of streets which make up the living town one finds the souks, with engaging salesmen luring the

visitor into their tiny shops and booths. Printed Egyptian cotton tablecloths, bales of cotton fabric, galebeahs of all materials and colours, brass and leatherwork and a good deal of hideous tourist souvenir stock of one kind or another are displayed. Some of the apparent ivory carvings are in fact made of plastic. You are expected to bargain, and may get the price down to half the opening offer. Personally I prefer the souks of Aswan, and the Khan el-Khalili in Cairo is of course much more extensive, but it is certainly worthwhile to stroll through those of Luxor.

An alternative for serious shopping is the group of shops in the arcades between the New Winter Palace Hotel and Luxor Temple. Here you will find high quality goods at fixed prices which obviate the problem of bargaining. There are large printed tablecloths; printed cotton dress material (many of the designs are based on ancient Egyptian wall paintings and some are beautiful); pictures painted on papyrus. There are books, too, carvings, copies of ancient pots, figurines, brass, handbags, jewellery and the typical Egyptian appliqué cloth pictures.

Hotels
The town has a number of hotels of every grade, 25 at least, of which half-a-dozen are worth mentioning for the foreign visitor. There is an excellent Hilton with very good food though some distance from the centre of the town, to the north not far from Karnak. The Isis is another good large hotel on the river bank to the south, and on the same side of the town along the river is a good Sheraton (which organises day cruises to Dendara). The Mövenpick Jolie Ville is a 'village' type luxury hotel on the Crocodile Island some kilometres to the south. All these are in the five-star range. The old classic Winter Palace Hotel rated four-star is now being refurbished. For really cheap accommodation try the two-star Mina Palace right in the centre of the corniche opposite the new Visitors' Centre; very simple and basic but widely used by British people who live and work in Egypt.

It is important to have advance reservations in Luxor, where the better hotels tend to be booked up far in advance right through the winter season and into April and even May.

Restaurants
Apart from the hotels the following are quite good: Marhaba Restaurant on the flat roof of the shops arcade building between Luxor Temple and the Winter Palace Hotel (tel. 382 633); Bodor Restaurant, which is a boat moored opposite the Winter Palace; and the simple New Karnak Restaurant near the railway station (tel. 382 427), popular with students.

Karnak

Once there was an avenue of stone ram-headed sphinxes lining the way from Luxor temple to Karnak, or to be exact from Karnak — which was founded much earlier — to Luxor. A large number remain at the entrance to Karnak.

Karnak is an enormous complex which overwhelms you by sheer size. It is claimed to be by far the largest place of worship in the world. Leonard Cottrell wrote with disarming honesty that to him the whole complex was as hideous as it is large. I certainly would not go so far as that. To me there is a very impressive majesty about this strange jumble of buildings, and much of the detailed work is superb — as Cottrell added. The magic of Karnak is again that indefinable mystery of ruins. For this great temple quarter was a city in itself. Among the buildings still to be seen there is a range in age of nearly 2,000 years, from the beginning of the Middle Kingdom, about 2000 BC right on to the time of Ptolemy Auletes half a century before Christ.

And today there is plenty of modern life too in the tourists who arrive at the gates of Karnak. Outside is the noisiest and most confusing crowd in Luxor. Of course, it is possible given time to make an independent visit at a less busy hour.

Great Temple of Amun

We pass between the two great sections of the entrance pylon (wall) built by the Ptolemies, on through the Great Court and into the Hypostyle Hall with its 134 columns, the central ones being 10 metres (33 feet) in circumference and 21 metres (69 feet) high. They are equal in size to Trajan's Column in Rome, erected some 1,300 years later.

Photographers wander about in an ecstasy of perplexity. Weary sightseers sit at the foot of the columns. One needs to stop and let this amazing place sink into the consciousness.

Beyond the hall and central court is the site of the original temple, but the whole area was the great temple of Amun himself, his official residence as it has been described, and all around within it are other temples, those of Ptah, of Khonsu, and of the deified Pharaohs: Seti II, Ramesses III, Amenhotep II, and a late Ptolemaic temple. There are courts, statues, colonnades, and to the south a sacred lake. In one place just inside the entrance, earth ramps remain against a wall showing how these vast constructions were carried out.

Today it is one huge rather confusing if evocative archaeological site. Some great parts of this temple world still stand to defy time and imagination. Some have fallen. Grass and stones and the all-pervading sand have penetrated where once all must have been smooth, polished, immaculate.

That is why time and the alchemy of quiet are needed. For it was here that Queen Hatshepsut held the reins of power more than 3,400 years ago and for some two decades ruled as a pharaoh — the only woman of the ancient dynasties to do so. A powerful character she must have been, and determined like other pharaohs to leave her marks for posterity.

She had two colossal obelisks, (the northern one still stands 30 metres (97 feet) high and weighs 323 tons) erected here in the temple area, sheathed in electrum (gold and silver alloy) to the honour of Amun, from whom, to legitimise her pharaonic position, she claimed divine descent. Her frustrated and enraged half-brother Tuthmosis III walled up and defaced her memorial after her death, but she has the final victory. He may have been the real founder of the great empire of the New Kingdom, but far more people have heard of Hatshepsut.

It must have been here too, in the following century, that Akhenaton had his vision of the one god, so that he moved his worship and centre of government to Tel el-Amarna, and to here that the orthodoxy of the time returned after his death.

Ramesses II of course bestrode the majesty of Karnak for even longer than Queen Victoria ruled England, proclaimed with the oft quoted 'Look on my works, ye mighty, and despair!' Ramesses III was the last great temple builder in Thebes.

From here at great festivals, the image of Amun was taken by barge to Luxor temple while processions of priests on land bore models of the sacred boat. In one small sanctuary in the temple of Ptah is the only remaining image of a deity — the goddess Sekhmet — with the body of a woman and the face of a lioness. It is all here, in mighty stone, in mural pictures, in hieroglyph records, and more than these perhaps in the strange spirit of the place.

Son et Lumière
One way to invoke the life is to attend the Son et Lumière performance, given daily. Like the one at the Giza Pyramids this is given in different languages; English daily except Sunday, but it is advisable to check on times and languages in case there are alterations. Most package tours which visit Luxor include this Son et Lumière, and it is an experience not to be missed. Tickets LE 10.

After dark Karnak has an even greater aura of size and mystery. The audience is guided to various different points among the ruins where lights, recorded voices and music recount and illustrate the history of the place and its people. The final part is given with the audience in tiers of seats above the sacred lake. One imaginative part of the script gives a vision of the long vanished living city, the wooden or mud houses, and the human lives, loves, dancing, marketing, the colour and the fabrics; all the transient things which time has eclipsed. Stark might and endeavour remain enshrined here, but it should not be forgotten that once there was also tenderness and frailty.

The Valleys of the Kings and Queens

Ferries cross from the east side regularly to the city of the dead which spreads back from the western bank of the Nile into bare, brown sandy hills. The crossing takes about five minutes and tickets for the temples and tombs should be purchased from the booth at the west bank dock. All the transportation on the farther side will be arranged for organised parties but, if you are alone, cars can be hired at the landing stage, and donkeys and bicycles are available.

Two points to be remembered are that with these charges and a car the cost of a visit to Thebes of the Dead is considerably higher than sightseeing on the Luxor side, and that it is a long and tiring morning's expedition, although immensely interesting. You cannot really omit the transport because the sites are widely scattered. Also the heat, especially in the Valley of the Kings can be intense, and there is no respite from it even when you enter the underground tombs. I remember noticing this even in December. In the royal tombs here the dry heat meets one like a powerful barrier in the semi-darkness. So — go early in the morning, and take your time. It is easy to spend a whole day on the west bank and there is a rest house where you can get refreshments. Here as much as anywhere in Egypt you need strong, comfortable shoes and a sun hat in the hotter months.

History
Ahmose, first king of the 18th Dynasty in the middle of the 16th century BC, built the last known pyramids at Abydos for himself and his grandmother, but these were memorials, their bodies being buried at Thebes. After that the pyramid form was abandoned and the pharaonic remains were sealed in rock tombs with separate funerary temples.

These temples were built at the very edge of the fertile region, and the tombs were cut into the side of the mountains themselves, in barren 'wadis' where it was hoped — misguidedly, as it proved — the famous dead and their treasures would be safely hidden from pillage.

This second city of the dead goes right back to the days when Thebes became capital of the united kingdom of Upper and Lower Egypt at the time of the 11th Dynasty, about 2000 BC. Apparently it was always kept as a great necropolis. There was a population on this side of the river in ancient times but they were all occupied in the industry of death: special priests, embalmers, workmen who carved out the tombs, and so on.

Colossi of Memnon
The first important sight is the pair of enormous seated pharaonic figures which are all that remain of the mortuary or funerary temple of Amenhotep III. The Greeks later named them the Colossi of Memnon. They stand in the green, cultivated strip of land which runs back from the Nile. Beyond to the west lie the mountains and tombs; behind them the great expanses of the Sahara.

Valley of the Kings
The tombs of 64 pharaohs have been discovered in the Valley of the Kings, and only one, that of Tutankhamun had not been robbed and emptied of its treasures in remote times. That is why that young pharaoh has become world famous and regarded as the epitome of the splendour of ancient Egypt. The treasures buried with him for his journey to eternity have now travelled the world: their permanent home is in the Egyptian Antiquities Museum in Cairo although the mummy of Tutankhamun himself with its golden mask remains in the tomb. But as your guide will tell you, his resting place is small compared with others, and probably only remained intact because that of Ramesses VI was built over it. The treasures of older and more famous pharaohs would have eclipsed his.

Temple of Hatshepsut in the Valley of the Kings

The largest tomb is that of Seti I, about 1300 BC, where there are very beautiful drawings and reliefs and a famous zodiac design on the ceiling. Others in the Valley of the Kings are those of Amenhotep III, Horemheb, Ramesses III and Ramesses VI.

The huge Ramesseum, mortuary temple of Ramesses II and the even larger one of Ramesses III known as Medinet Habu (which actually includes an earlier temple built by Amenhotep I and a later one dating from 700 BC) are other outstanding sites. An hour or two can be devoted individually to these, and to Deir el-Bahari.

Temple of Hatshepsut
Deir el-Bahari is the mortuary temple of Queen Hatshepsut and quite unlike anything else in Thebes. Here as elsewhere, she was determined to immortalise her name and though Tuthmosis III had many of the wall pictures defaced in his efforts to obliterate her memory the building remains, nobly sited with cliffs as a background to its colonnades and terraces. The architect Senmut, believed to be the Queen's lover, included a picture of himself and a love message in the temple, discreetly hidden behind a door. He and Hatshepsut planned this temple as a 'paradise' and pictures on its walls show the expeditions sent to the distant land of Punt (probably Somalia) to bring back exotic trees and animals to adorn it.

Valley of the Queens
South west lies the Valley of the Queens where more than 50 tombs have been discovered but few are open to the public. The most important are those of Queen Nefertari favourite wife of Ramesses II, and of Queen Titi. Princes were also buried here: one of the well known tombs is that of Amenherkhepshef, the 12-year-old son of Ramesses III.

Tombs of the Nobles
Another area is that of the Tombs of the Nobles. These are in scattered groups along the edge of the desert. Strikingly smaller than the great pharaohs' mausoleums they are still very interesting and some have wonderful wall drawings. Probably the most famous and most frequently visited is that of Nakht, described by guides as minister of agriculture, or more gracefully and officially as 'Scribe of the Granaries' to Tuthmosis IV. Other important ones are those of Rekhmire-Re, Vizier to Tuthmosis III, and Ramose, Vizier to Akhenaton.

Temple of Philae

Up the Nile: Luxor to Aswan

Sitting on deck at Luxor as the sun goes down, there is a fascinating sense of being moored between two worlds in several different senses. Across the darkening water the fiery disc sinks behind the mountains, dark with their still only partially revealed mysteries of the ancient dead. The sky pales from pink and gold to lemon, and the palm trees are sharply silhouetted. There is the lively but faintly nostalgic tinkling sound of carriage bells as the horses clip-clop smartly along the corniche. The remote past and a quaintly unreal present are welded together by triumphant nature. Even this moment belongs to the past, for tomorrow we sail southwards in our small floating hotel, deeper into Africa and a sense of primeval things.

It is very pleasant relaxing on the deck of one of these Nile cruise boats. There is an awning to shade you from the intense heat of the sun by day, plenty of deck chairs, and a bar which is open when the passengers most require it, before lunch and in the evening.

There are only two drawbacks to sitting on deck, one is the wind at certain seasons of the year, the other is the mosquitoes. Not even the river will safeguard one from the sand and dust during the khamseen winds which may blow for several days in March or April, making the sky grey and sometimes whipping up real sandstorms. Still, it was during the khamseen that I actually saw the colour of the Nile water. 'Eau de Nil' has been a fashion colour for generations of couturiers and I had always thought of it as something of a romantic fancy. I can now bear witness that that is the genuine colour of the Nile!

Cruise ships

There are more than 100 cruise ships in service on the Nile and the number increases every year. Some details of different operating firms are given in General Information. I have no hesitation in saying that by far the most comfortable, and I think enjoyable, way of seeing at least the 'classic' cruise section of the Nile, the 225 kilo-metres (140 miles) from Luxor up to Aswan or vice versa is on one of these ships. Like any other cruise, you have the advantage of taking your accommodation with you. If by any bad luck you are tired or not well you can opt out of the day's programme and still reach your final destination. For at least the number of days on board you will not sit in airports, or be herded on and off coaches either as a member of a group or individually. You will not have punctures or lose your way. Provided you are on board it does not matter in the least whether the ship sails half an hour late or at what time it reaches its destination. You can eat and drink and sleep and talk or watch the scenery without the slightest reference to a detailed travel schedule, and all that is very soothing to the nerves.

On this particular occasion I was on one of the smaller cruise vessels with 24 cabins taking a maximum of 48 passengers, which is a reasonable number for the sightseeing trips ashore. The ship's officers, crew and stewards were Egyptian and the cruise organisa-tion personnel Spanish. All spoke enough English to present no difficulties, and there was an English-speaking guide and comparable guides for passengers of other languages. This ship may be said to be typical of these smaller Nile ships and provides an easy 'popular' type of cruise, as distinct from the more serious, archaeologically orientated ones which carry well-known experts as guide lecturers. The cruise formed part of a complete package which included a few days' stay in Cairo at the beginning and end of the holiday. There are others which you can book through Cairo firms and which are simply Nile holidays and can therefore be fitted into an independently planned tour of Egypt. The river boats operated by the Hilton Hotels are very luxurious, as are those owned by the Sheraton Hotels.

One of the advantages of travelling on the river is the freedom from dust. Egypt is a dry dusty country, and being surrounded by water is restful, for this reason, quite apart from the gentle speed of travel and the peace. It is by no means always cooler; indeed there are few places hotter than the open deck in full sunlight, but there is a sort of aesthetic coolness.

Gently the ship forges ahead upstream. In this direction the first section up to Esna will probably be made at night. On a downstream cruise you pass along the broad river with fields and palm trees and some villages on the banks. By road the distance is only about 50 kilometres (31 miles) and there are trains on the main Nile railway line by which a day trip from Luxor to Esna is feasible. There are also coach excursions from Luxor.

On the river one comes to the first barrage or dam shortly before Esna, the ship going into a lock through which it rises to the upper level. The lock of course provides a flurry of activity. Here we are side by side with a long, shabby barge whose tall, dark-skinned, white-haired skipper climbs along the narrow planking beside his deckhouse cabin carrying a bright green plastic bucket. He is apparently preparing a meal while his craft is penned inside the lock.

Above, as we reach the upstream level there is another cruise ship and several smaller boats waiting to go down. Along the quay to which they are moored, a row of vendors are inviting trade with the passengers on deck. They are a colourful band, mostly young but wearing the traditional garb, the majority in thin, long sky-blue galebeahs, others in pale green or white; all except the young boys wear turbans. The faces are thin, dark, handsome and often bearded. They are selling beads and trinkets of various sorts, and Coptic crosses, and they toss them up to interested customers. One man is a snake charmer, performing with his cobra on the quayside.

Esna

Esna is a busy country town on the west bank of the river, about 58 kilometres (36 miles) south of Luxor. There are horse carriages but it is only a short walk and more fun to go on foot through the small streets and souk. The speciality to buy here is a kind of black net overdress worn by the women and decorated with gold and silver sequins or spangles. This dress is by no means limited to Esna; you will see the same in other places, but the town claims it by right as an Esna product. I do not know whether the claim is true, and in any case to me the garment is not particularly attractive, though it might appeal to westerners for fancy dress. Otherwise I think the work would look rather garish in the cool grey daylight of western Europe. There are, however, some rather pretty little triangles of black net which are used as a head covering with a row of small gold or silver discs along one side which is worn over the forehead.

The souk of Esna is not very picturesque, some of the stalls are like those of an open-air western market, but you can get some attractive printed cotton goods such as the large tablecloths, some with sets of napkins, and decorated with pharaonic designs which you may be able to bargain down to LE 20, and some very good printed galebeahs. In thin cotton you may get these for LE 15, but the better ones will cost up to twice as much. A three-metre cotton dress length may be bought for LE 10 by long and amiable negotiation.

Esna Temple

Esna temple is encrusted with the modern town, indeed one can well believe that there is far more to be discovered underneath the modern dwellings. Much excavation has been needed to reveal the part we can see. You climb down as into a great pit to find the temple of Khnum, described as the creator-god who shaped men from Nile clay. The present building is Ptolemaic, an example of the decline in true Egyptian art which came with the Greek domination, but there was an earlier temple here dating from about 1500 BC, the time of Tuthmosis III, that vindictive half-brother of Hatshepsut. That has gone, however, and this structure is probably no earlier than 180 BC and was completed much later, about AD 250 by the Romans. The Emperor Decius is mentioned on one of the reliefs.

The latest representations of a pharaoh were discovered here. Over some of the temple doors are carved vultures, always a symbol of power in Upper Egypt and shown here to drive away evil spirits. After the uniting of the two kingdoms the pharaohs wore on their crowns the vulture of Nekeb for Upper Egypt and the symbol of Wadjet of Buto, a serpent-goddess of Lower Egypt. In the same way the two flower symbols of lotus (Upper Egypt) and papyrus (Lower Egypt) were combined. A guide once told me that in Esna the vulture is still considered lucky. She pointed upwards from the temple area where we stood and there on the walls of a modern shop and apartment block was a vulture device.

Nekeb

Nekeb, the actual cult centre for the vulture goddess Nekhebt was on the eastern bank of the Nile farther upstream, between Esna and Edfu where the village of El-Kâb now stands. In the same area was Nekhen (now El-Kom-el-Ahmar), where the hawk god Horus was worshipped. Little is to be seen of either today but before the kingdoms were joined and even in the days of the early dynasties, these were among the most important religious centres of Upper Egypt.

Above Esna there is a richly fertile stretch of irrigated land on both banks. The palm trees are thick, life appears to be hard but placid; the noisy, cosmopolitan world of Cairo is very, very far away.

Edfu

Some 50 kilometres (31 miles) south from Esna you come to Edfu, a small and somewhat shabby town on the west bank of the river. Its temple is one of the famous sights of the Nile valley and the tourist cruise ships have clearly introduced an important if limited source of income to a place where living is hard and the cultivated land is restricted to a seven-mile wide strip along the Nile.

The contrast between this luxury industry bringing foreigners and the remote little town is striking. When we arrived there were four other ships already moored to the steep sandy bank, two of the 'large' Sheraton ones, and two others of about the same size as ours, but the passengers were already at the temple, and the open street by the river was quiet.

I clambered up the bank and strolled along it, collecting a knot of eager children who ran beside me asking for baksheesh and cigarettes. A group of men was sitting in front of a café. One shouted to the children to leave me in peace which they did, rather regretfully. For the rest, there was a strong smell of the goats who search so diligently for food in unlikely places. Two little black kids trotted along with their mother, and there were several tired looking donkeys, one or two with open sores. Edfu is a rather sad looking place.

Edfu Temple
The temple lies some little distance from the river, further back in the town, and the journey is made by a short drive in the familiar calèches. On arrival the visitors clamber down, pick their way through the mêlée of carriages while — as at Karnak — the drivers repeat their numbers to you for the return journey. There is an entrance gate, an open space inside with souvenir stalls and a tree or two, and behold! — the great size and importance of Edfu's temple.

Like Esna it is Ptolemaic, but instead of climbing down as one does there to see what is now below ground level, Edfu temple stands towering and magnificent, high above town and river. It was built in the 3rd century BC though additions continued until 57 BC. Thanks to the French Egyptologist Mariette, who succeeded in clearing its terraces of modern dwellings more than a century ago, it is in a remarkable state of preservation, huge and awe inspiring, giving perhaps the most striking impression remaining to us of what Egypt's ancient places of worship were like in their heyday.

There are two great pylons, a forecourt with massive columns, two hypostyle halls and beyond them the smaller vestibules and a sanctuary. On one side there is a cliff below and beyond, green fields of crops, palm trees and a Moslem cemetery. A little group of women swathed in black veils and galebeahs walk through the fields. Here and there are the ubiquitous donkeys: the rural life is timeless.

The proportions of this temple are superb, the art of its decorations, carvings and reliefs is less important, being of the late, Ptolemaic time, but very interesting for what they portray. It was dedicated to the god Horus, orginally part of the sun god cult but later combined with that other Horus who was the son of Osiris and Isis. It was linked in worship with the temple of Hathor at Dendara (161 kilometres, 100 miles north), and the new year (July 19) celebrations included processions carrying the image of Horus all the way to Dendara — some 150 kilometres (93 miles) by land — and that of Hathor, Horus' wife, back to visit Edfu.

Some people from the surrounding countryside are said still to come here by night to worship the ancient gods in secret.

Kom Ombo

The last stopping place on these cruises and only 50 kilometres (31 miles) short of Aswan is Kom Ombo. Unlike the other sites it is a temple standing alone with no town or village surrounding it. The ship moors at the sandy eastern bank, and visitors climb the gangplank to be met by a hopeful group of smiling vendors carrying armfuls of galebeahs, tablecloths, bead chains and postcards, and take a path leading round the shoulder of a low sandy hill, the temple towering above.

It is a beautiful spot, with proud ruins overlooking a peaceful bend of the Nile. Here are the gold of sand and stone, blue sky, and some green born of the marriage of earth and water. A felucca moves gently on the river, its sails just filled.

On this site there may have been very early sanctuaries. Certainly in the New Kingdom, temples were built by Amenhotep I, Tuthmosis III and Ramesses II, but all are now gone. Once again what we see is the work of the Ptolemies added to by the Romans. The emperors Tiberius, Domitian, Geta and Caracalla all had a hand in it.

The temple had a dual dedication, to Haroeris who was another manifestation of the hawk god and is described as the 'Elder Horus', and Sobek the crocodile god who will be remembered from El Fayoum. The two had equal status here, and we can see their two forecourts, two hypostyle halls, two sets of vestibules and two sanctuaries. However, in the time of the 18th Dynasty — the New Kingdom between 1500 and 1300 BC — the temple then standing on the site was called Per-Sobek (House of Sobek) so it may be that Sobek was then pre-eminent.

In one small chamber there is a number of mummified crocodiles. In another place there is a panel depicting surgical instruments. Despite sun, wind and sand there is still colour in the surviving ceiling paintings and on the heads of some of the columns.

Aswan

Above Kom Ombo the valley and its cultivated region narrows until we come to Aswan itself and the first of the six cataracts on the Nile. This is traditionally a meeting point both geographical and historical. It was the ancient frontier between Egypt and Nubia, the cataract forming the first great natural barrier on a river journey from Lower Egypt.

In those days the city at this focal point was called To-Seti and it was built on what is still known as Elephantine Island. It was a great trading centre for the ancients: gold and ivory, semi-precious stones, minerals, slaves, and the local granite which was used in so many of the pharaonic temples downstream and even found its way across to Arabia and the Mediterranean — all were sold or bartered here. And again today the High Dam and the developments associated with it make Aswan the meeting place of past and present in Upper Egypt.

The people are Nubians. Already far downstream in Luxor and the smaller places we have visited, the Nubian influence has been strong in the people, who are quite unlike the mixed inhabitants of Lower Egypt. This is a striking race, black skinned, with handsome features, tall, well built and very upright; a proud and independent people essentially belonging to this north-east corner of the continent and entirely different from the tribes of central Africa or the Arabs and coastal peoples of the north.

As at all Nile towns, the cruise ships moor along the river front of Aswan which stands on the east bank with a broad corniche road backed by shops and offices. Here we shall leave the cruise, though actual passengers will use it as their hotel while staying here. Many more visitors will arrive by other routes, road or train: air is the most usual method for foreigners. The airport is on the opposite, western side and is reached by a road across the Dam.

Up the Nile: Luxor to Aswan

There is a danger on package tours that Aswan itself is squeezed into a half day when one is very tired after a long morning's air excursion to Abu Simbel. That has happened once to me, and it is a pity, for there is quite a lot to see here, and even more to assimilate and understand. Luxor's glory is wholly dependent on the pharaonic times, but Aswan is a mixture of many ages, moods and forces. So if at all possible give a couple of days to this city.

The principal sights of Aswan are: Elephantine Island, the Unfinished Obelisk, the Temple of Philae, the Tombs of the Nobles, the Mausoleum of the Aga Khan, the Botanical Gardens, the original Aswan Dam, and the city's modern pride and joy, the High Dam.

Temples and Museum

There are various remains of temples here. At the entrance to one is a likeness of Alexander II dressed like an ancient Egyptian pharaoh, presenting offerings to the gods (one is reminded of some of London's statues where 19th century statesmen are depicted in Roman togas). Another temple is that of Ptolemy VII, dating from the 2nd century BC. The pharaohs Seti I and Ramesses II figure in others. Also on Elephantine Island is the Aswan Museum with its special collection of antiquities from this region and Nubia, and there is the Aswan Nilometer which recorded the levels of the ancient flood waters, and by which the early scientists were able to evaluate the food production of the land.

Everyone goes to see the Unfinished Obelisk, partly because of its great size and partly because it still lies in one of the quarries where much of Aswan's famous granite was excavated. This colossal piece 40 metres (131 feet) long and estimated to weigh 1,168 tons, proved to have a flaw when the work was far advanced, and so was left in situ. Your guide may tell you it was being cut for Queen Hatshepsut, but I do not know whether there is evidence for this. The Romans had another try with it, then evidently gave up.

Temple of Philae

The Temple of Philae is on an island between the two great dams. It dates from the end of the pharaonic period, 4th century BC, and was dedicated to Isis. After the Aswan Dam was constructed in 1902 most of the temple was almost always submerged. With the building of the High Dam 50 years later and the threat of total submersion, it was decided to move the whole construction to the safety of another island, Agilkia. This was an operation of great importance, but one which has been overshadowed by the gargantuan work at Abu Simbel.

It is a beautiful place, and peaceful if you can escape the crowds. Rose coloured oleanders were in bloom, and a dove was cooing in the trees when I walked round the temple alone. But it was August, and the temperature 102°F. The entrance charge is LE 4, and boats to take you across and back charge LE 10 for up to 8 people. Son et Lumière performances are given in English, Spanish, French, German, Italian and Arabic. English daily except Sunday and Thursday. Tickets LE 10. A taxi to take you from the town to the boat station (daytime), wait one hour and return, should not cost more than LE 15.

Tombs of the Nobles
The tombs of the nobles are on the opposite, west side of the river. They are cut into the cliff face and go back to the late part of the Old Kingdom, 6th to 8th Dynasties, about 2300 BC. They are not architecturally exciting but some fascinating inscriptions have been deciphered from their walls describing the achievements and journeys of those who were buried there.

Aga Khan's Mausoleum
In our own time, the late Aga Khan III (Sir Sultan Mohamed Shah) had a great love for Aswan and when he died in the late 1950s he was buried here. The simple, very beautiful mausoleum is on a hill behind the villa on the west bank where he lived when he came to Egypt. His widow, the Begum, still lives in Aswan for part of the year, but whether she is there or not her personal gift of a single red rose is placed on her husband's tomb every day. The mausoleum can be visited daily, except Mondays, 0900-1700.

Monastery of St Simon
Behind this, a path leads to the ruins of the 6th century Coptic Monastery of St Simon, a 15 minute walk away. This was occupied by monks for over 300 years, and pilgrims still come here. Some of the frescoes of Christ and the Apostles can be seen, as well as monks' cells, the refectory and kitchens, millstones, washing places, and a place for making sacramental wine.

Kitchener's Island
The Botanical Garden is on an island once the property of Kitchener when he was British Consul-General in Egypt, known both as Kitchener's and Plantation Island. This is a peaceful, pleasant place with a number of tropical trees and flowers and many rare plants.

Aswan High Dam
Rightly, it is often pointed out that the structural landmarks of Egypt's history are colossal: the Pyramids, Sphinx, the temples of Abu Simbel are the symbols of pharaonic times. Now the advance of the country into modern times is marked by another, the High Dam.

Any journey up the Nile will show the visitor that the people of the river have been concerned through the ages, vitally and actively, with the control of its waters. The ancient floods drew life and crops from the parched land. By natural or artificial methods of irrigation the fertile valley was maintained, and in some cases water was carried across the desert by canal to extend or create oases, as at El Fayoum. Because the extent of natural flooding varied, the ancient Egyptians developed quite extraordinary scientific methods of measuring and gauging the flow, to prepare for drought years, to safeguard the people and civilisation.

Aswan is the obvious natural point for major control. The visitor will find a striking contrast in the appearance of the river here, when compared with Luxor. Gone is the broad, calm, purposeful stream flowing between low green shores or sandy banks. Here the town is built just below the cataract, the last point at which a ship can be manoeuvred and moored. Immediately above are the rocks and falls of water, the stony pathway of the river with a thousand little splashing waterfalls. The river bulges and is dotted with islands.

Following the great engineering feat of the Suez Canal in the mid 19th century came the Aswan Dam in 1902, and now in our own time the vast project of the High Dam, completed in 1971, which has been constructed seven kilometres (four miles) upstream of the old one. When you visit the Dam — about 10 kilometres (six miles) from town — you go first to the exhibition building where there is a model of the whole operation, as well as pictures and maps. Then you can drive round to see the actual construction site. Allow at least an hour to do justice to the Dam.

The broad principle of the whole thing is that a diversion channel was cut in the east bank of the Nile and the rock removed in doing this was used for the foundation of the great dam itself. This is four kilometres (2¼ miles) long, and 107 metres (360 feet) high, built of earth, rock and concrete and is one of the largest dams in the world, producing 10 billion kilowatts electricity an hour. Since its completion, the waters of the Nile have been diverted through the special channel and tunnels, where their flow is controlled. The whole face of Upper Egypt has been changed by this, with the creation of the vast Nasser Lake. The project cost a billion dollars and was carried out with aid from Russia and Russian experts, though the actual construction work was done with Egyptian labour. It provided work for some 35,000 men.

Not everyone will find the High Dam exciting. If you come to Egypt with eyes and ears only for antiquities then this huge modern barrage may seem an anachronism, but it is in fact very much a vital part of the whole pattern of a living country.

Kalabsha and Beit-al-Wali
Another of the buildings rescued from the devouring waters of the

new lake is the Kalabsha Temple, a Roman temple built in the reign of the Emperor Octavius Augustus (30 BC-AD 14) and a good example of the adoption of ancient Egyptian architectural styles by the Roman colonists. Originally it stood on the west bank of the Nile 55 kilometres (34 miles) south of Aswan. It was completely dismantled and has been re-erected near the High Dam. Another temple in the High Dam area is that known as Beit-al-Wali which was carved out of the rocks in the time of Ramesses II, and much later was used as a Coptic church.

One of the most delightful parts of a visit to Aswan is sailing in feluccas on the town reach below the cataract. There are feluccas — the immemorial Nile sailing boats — at Cairo, Luxor and other places on the river, but here there is the added charm of the smaller islands and the changing views as the boat moves gently among them, either for a trip in its own right or as a means of transport from islands to shore, or across the river. Enquire at the tourist office for the right charges.

Aswan Town
Wandering through the town is also pleasant. Behind the corniche street of Aswan with its rather ugly shops and offices other streets extend into the heart of the town. Some are quite wide busy thoroughfares, others narrow and crowded, linked by little paths and alleys. After dusk this is to me the most absorbing side of the whole place, for much of the trade is concerned with the natural day to day life of the people rather than with wooing tourists. Aswan is a highlight for holiday-makers and the southernmost base in a tour of Upper Egypt but, unlike Luxor, tourism is not its sole important industry.

Here the locals are out for an evening stroll, the younger women looking with as much interest as the visitor at bales of cloth displayed in the narrow, open-fronted shops of the souks. Others are buying food, meat, vegetables, pots and pans and brightly coloured plastic pails and bowls. The spice stalls are always fascinating with their delicate, elusive scents. The Aswan spice shops are particularly good and varied, their wares displayed in neat little open bags like miniature sacks of grain. You can buy in any quantity by weight. Today they also offer ground spices in cellophane packages, less picturesque but more convenient for the traveller to take home, and the contents will, I think, always be freshly ground and packed because there is a big local trade in spices. You can get real saffron here, and such relative rarities as the grey, twisted sticks of root ginger. There are also little pyramids of a deep blue powder used in washing to whiten clothes – like the old English 'blue-bag'.

As the darkness comes down with a southern swiftness more people join the throng. Lights hanging above stall or shop fronts throw dark shadows among the buildings. Shabbiness disappears and one is caught up in the moving pattern of a community. Women never frequent the simple, open-air street cafés, where grave, turbanned men sit at the little tables. There are a few tiny glasses of tea or cups of coffee on the table, but for the most part they seem to sit there without providing much trade for the owner, often playing dominoes or shatterang, a form of chess.

The whole essence of wandering in Egyptian towns is to follow up a glimpse of traditional life, a picturesque building or to turn into an attractive shop. To follow your own instinct or interest. Aswan is not so large that one can get seriously lost, and if you keep a sense of where the river lies you can return to the corniche in a few minutes.

One main shopping street runs parallel to the Nile and in one section contains the souk of most interest to visitors who are looking for things to buy. There are excellent leather goods, belts and bags and the tooled leather covers for 'pouffes', which can be bought and taken home folded and flat, to be filled later. There is a wide range of jewellery, brass and ornaments and knick-knacks of all kinds, as well as cotton goods, bales of printed material, galebeahs, tablecloths, and the rest.

There are many opportunities for the photographer, here as elsewhere. The locals will understand if you take pictures of them selling their wares, or with donkeys or boats, or outside well-known buildings. Where you want to photograph children or a carriage or any obvious part of a trader's calling, then you should give them your custom or baksheesh as is appropriate. But a sense of courtesy and human dignity should restrain one from the constant clicking of cameras where the scene is personal or pathetic: an old woman, swathed in draperies, dozing on a step, or a blind man walking through the street with his hand on a child's shoulder.

It is in these streets that you move among the people themselves. The westerner cannot sink unnoticed into the crowd. Our faces and our clothes make us conspicuous, but we can pass through this world and learn much, remembering that it is better to smile than to stare, and that it is important to appear interested chiefly in the legitimate ploys of the tourist — such as shopping.

Long ago I abandoned photography for a variety of reasons but acquired the habit of committing certain living pictures to memory, and I commend it to the traveller in Egypt where one sees many vivid characteristic scenes which cannot be captured by camera. In one alleyway you will see the inmates of a stable; two donkeys and a horse, perhaps, and a man taking off their harness. The interior is dimly lit, the floor beaten earth. All stables in the Middle

East are the same, and one has a sudden vision of what another stable looked like, 2,000 years ago in Bethlehem.

On one visit to Aswan I saw another picture which has remained in my mind, clear in every detail. Darkness had fallen as I passed the open front of a smithy. An electric forge was working — it had modern equipment — and the sparks stabbed the air. One older man and two young ones were at work, white turbanned, their blue and green galebeahs falling in folds round tall, spare figures and the dark faces, one lined and all bearded, were calmly intent. The elderly man raised his arm to point to some object and for a moment looked like a prophet of old. The square open front framed the picture, which had a strange quality of glowing, timeless life. I walked slowly past, trying not to stare, made a circle through some neighbouring alleys and got another glimpse on my return, the position of the figures slightly changed, before I walked away softly into the darkness.

Hotels

In the winter, Aswan is very popular with tourists and it is advisable to book hotel rooms well in advance. At the moment, Aswan has some 19 hotels in all grades. The classic one is the five-star Cataract Hotel. Built originally in 1899, all Aswan's famous visitors of this century stayed here (there is an Agatha Christie suite). The hotel was taken over in 1986 by Pullman International Hotels, and restored to it's former glory. It stands on the east bank of the Nile looking towards Elephantine Island, is only a few minutes walk from the town and is now one of the very best hotels in Egypt. Other five-star hotels are the Oberoi Aswan on Elephantine Island, the New Cataract (also Pullman, a modern building), and the Tut Amun Village.

Two four-star hotels are the Amun on Amun Island (not to be confused with the Tut Amun mentioned above) and the Kalabsha Hotel, while the two-star Abu Simbel on the corniche and near the tourist office provides excellent value.

Most visitors eat in the hotels, but Egyptian gourmets go to the El Masri Restaurant: a very simple setting but first class food. There is a café in the Botanical Garden where it is pleasant to drink tea or soft drinks, and one or two other cafés as well as those belonging to the Rowing Club and the Police Club.

From Aswan, it is possible to travel south to Sudan by boat, but not by air. These boats take you the full length of Lake Nasser to Wadi Halfa and return the same day. Sailings are on Tuesdays and Saturdays. Single fare (approx.) LE 130 first class, LE 80 second class.

Rock Temple of Ramesses II, Abu Simbel

Lake Nasser and Abu Simbel

Abu Simbel lies at the upper end of Lake Nasser, 280 kilometres (173 miles) south of Aswan at a point where you are already far into Africa, within the tropical belt and close to Egypt's southern frontier with the Sudan.

Psychologically it is a pity that Abu Simbel is reached so easily by air and that most visitors make the trip in this way. There is almost

Right: Statue at Karnak, Abercrombie and Kent
Overleaf: The God Horus at Edfu (top left)
            Statue of Ramesses at the
            smaller Abu Simbel Temple (top right)
            Sinai Valley (bottom)

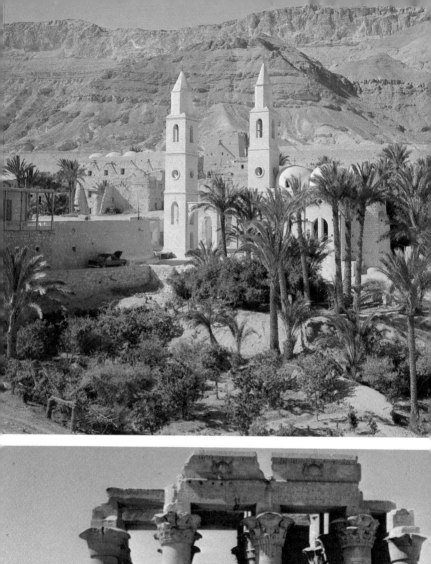

a shuttle air service between Aswan and Abu Simbel, with daily flights in each direction and certain through services to and from Cairo. The flying time from Aswan is 40 minutes or less. This air journey is as unromantic as any other short flight, though if you get a window seat the deep blue waters of the lake are visible, its banks following the contours of the ancient hills and the surface sprinkled with islands which were once hills too. Yet the visitor has little chance to realise that he is flying over history still in the making. For those willing to face a long hot drive it is now possible to travel from Aswan to Abu Simbel by bus or service (shared) taxi. Details from Aswan Tourist Office.

Lake Nasser

If the High Dam is a vast construction using more material than many pyramids, the lake it has created is something far more revolutionary, for here man has mastered nature on a mighty scale and by this one great practical and symbolic act, Egypt moved into the modern world. The project was of course designed to increase the irrigated area of the country: to provide power and to maintain water supplies which would draw on this, one of the world's great reservoirs, in years when the Nile's flow — fed by rains in eastern Africa — fell below average. One might say that it was the culmination of the work of the mathematicians and hydrologists of the pharaohs, Greeks, Romans and Arabs in their varying degrees. And it has succeeded. The lake is in full operation, and has brought an entirely new means of life and development to Upper Egypt.

It has also brought a measure of change to the whole country, not always for the good. Much of this must have been foreseen by the original planners, though some of the results only became apparent in practice. The whole question is whether on balance the advantages outweigh the damage, and of course what the extent and effect of such damage will eventually prove to be.

At present while there is great official pride and also personal pride and satisfaction in the huge economic and life-saving asset which the lake provides, it is also used as a scapegoat for all plausible and implausible changes in the climate and the land. Nasser Lake gets the blame for anything from creeping damp in the temple of Esna to higher humidity, and certainly some of this may be true. To create a vast sheet of water where none existed throughout history and prehistory must affect the balance of nature. A few years ago a long-term European resident of Aswan told me that whereas

Previous page: *Bread making. Hutchison Library*
             Shaving. Hutchison Library
Left: *St Catherine's Monastery, Mount Sinai*
             Ptolemaic temple at Kom Ombo

in his early years there he remembered no rain at all, now a few drops fall occasionally!

The really major change in the lower Nile is the lack of perennial deposits of silt. The full meaning of Egypt being the gift of the Nile was that not only water but also rich fertile silt is carried down by the river. The traditional system of 'basin irrigation' by which the natural floods were channelled onto the surrounding land, and crops grown during the brief season when the floods subsided leaving moisture in the deposited rich mud, has been superseded by 'perennial irrigation' from the lake's reserves of water. But the silt now settles in the lake itself, and artificial fertilizers are being used on the land.

Abu Simbel

Abu Simbel's little airport is almost wholly a tourist one. Planeloads of visitors walk out of it, blinking in the fierce glare of the sun, climb into coaches or taxis and are driven in about 15 minutes to a point from which the temples are a five-minute walk.

Immediately below are the shining waters of the lake, all around are rough sandhills and a few bushes. The crowds of visitors and the inevitable sellers of souvenirs add touches of bright colour; a little human oasis in a world totally remote and rather unreal, though one passes through a village on the way from the airport. A path leads round the shoulder of a low hill and you climb downwards to an open space at the edge of the water. Here rough grass has been sown and there are a few trees. In spring at least there is a carpet of green, and turning inwards from the lake one is faced by the stark, red gold stone of Ramesses II's greatest legacy of immortality.

Abu Simbel Temple
Abu Simbel's main temple is the largest of all Egypt's colossal places of worship, and is of one period only, being the ultimate manifestation of Ramesses II's long reign. It stands on the west bank of the lake with its great carved figures and entrance facing east to the rising sun.

The temple is dedicated to three deities, Ptah of the underworld who was worshipped at Memphis, Amun of Thebes and a form of Horus, the sun god Ra-Harakhte. Outside, however, it is Ramesses himself and his family who dominate the great red sandstone façade. There are four huge seated figures of Ramesses, two on each side of the entrance and all more than 20 metres (66 feet) high. On the left of the second one there is also a figure of his mother Queen Ti and on the right one of Queen Nefertari his favourite wife. There are also representations of Amun and Ra-Harakhte though certainly not so striking or large as those of the pharaoh.

On the south wall an inscription records a peace treaty between the Egyptians and the Hittites, and it is pointed out as of special interest because it is the earliest known treaty of the kind.

Inside, the temple extends straight back for 61 metres (200 feet) and was originally cut from solid rock. You come first into the great hypostyle hall where there are eight columns backing enormous statues of Ramesses representing the god Osiris. The interior is dark, though light pours in through the entrance, but the darkness has probably helped to preserve the colours of the ceiling and wall paintings, which are very fine. Leading off from the side walls are some small storage rooms, also with wall decorations.

Moving still deeper into the cliff westwards, you come into a second, much smaller hall, 11 by 8 metres (36 by 26 feet) with four pillars and wall reliefs of Ramesses and Nefertari burning incense and some remarkably vital scenes of the pharaoh's horsemen and chariots.

Beyond this again is the sanctuary, the holy of holies which has four seated statues of Ramesses and the three gods of the temple dedication. The temple was so constructed that twice a year on the days of equinox the rising sun cast its rays right through the entrance to illuminate these figures.

Temple of Hathor
Just beyond this temple to the north is a smaller, simpler one dedicated to Hathor, also carved from solid rock. Ramesses had this made for Nefertari. Outside are six statues, four of the pharaoh, two of the queen and smaller ones of their children. The hypostyle hall has six columns with likenesses of Hathor, and at the back of the temple there are some beautiful reliefs of Nefertari and the goddess.

This, then, is Abu Simbel, a place extraordinary by any standards and well qualified to rank as one of the wonders of the world. One historian, H. R. Hall, called the temples 'gigantic abominations', others have found them some of the most remarkable buildings in the world. Certainly they are more personal than most of Egypt's other monuments for from them one can learn much of Ramesses II. Thinking of the huge figures of his creation here and at Thebes and Memphis, Hermann Kees wrote 'The colossus is, nevertheless, a true creation of his mind.' Come to Abu Simbel and judge for yourself. No description in words, not even photographs or paintings can capture the feeling of the place.

This is partly due to the subsequent history of the temples. For an aeon of time they were lost to the world in a shroud of sand and silence. Then more than a century and a half ago they were dis-

Lake Nasser and Abu Simbel

covered by an Italian explorer called Belzoni. Through the 19th century, intrepid travellers went there to see and wonder.

Saving Abu Simbel

When the great decision to create Nasser Lake was made, much of great archaeological importance had to be sacrificed to the needs of a living nation. There were many temples along the banks of the Nubian Nile, but those at Abu Simbel were the greatest and most famous, and the world took a hand in saving them. Through UNESCO the Egyptian government appealed to other governments, archaeological foundations, cultural institutions, schools, universities and individuals. Fifty nations contributed and 20 groups of people came to work in the valley before the gathering waters overwhelmed its treasures. Almost 30 different temples and monuments were dismantled and re-erected elsewhere.

The greatest salvage operation of all, Abu Simbel, was started in 1963, took nine years and cost 36 million dollars. A wall was built round the temples to protect them while the work was being done. Then the two temples which were carved from solid rock were literally cut out and cut up into great square blocks, the whole being reassembled like a child's puzzle on a new site 180 metres (600 feet) farther back and 64 metres (210 feet) above its old position; an operation which involved incredible precision and enormous power for the total weight of stone moved was 400,000 tons.

But more was needed to create the new setting. There was not a comparable hill at the right height, nor could huge holes have been excavated, so artificial hills were built round the temples to enclose them in the original way. Driving towards the site you will see these rather curious beehive-like hills in the distance which prove to be the outer shell of the reborn temples. When you have explored the depths of the great temple you are taken through another door, up wooden stairs and along catwalks and galleries to inspect the back, the concrete skin which supports the original interior walls inside the hollow artificial hill as a glass vacuum flask is suspended inside its protective casing. This, like the High Dam, is an amazing engineering achievement which will probably be the highlight of interest for some visitors, while others may find it disillusioning.

Among the thousands of visitors who come to Abu Simbel every year only a very small proportion stay overnight. That is understandable: a visit of a couple of hours will suffice to see the two temples and the technical devices which have ensured their survival. Time is usually at a premium in the tourist schedule and Egypt is a rich treasure house. Here there is, in archaeological terms, nothing more to see.

Add this to the fact that Abu Simbel is a convenient half day or even whole day optional extension trip from Aswan, and the general pattern is self evident. Fly from Cairo to Abu Simbel via Aswan, return to Aswan the same day and then take the great Nile valley route by easy stages via river or road. Or follow the same itinerary in reverse.

Village and Hotel

Nonetheless you can stay at Abu Simbel and I would recommend at least one night there for anyone who can afford the luxury of a little extra time. It is just because there is 'nothing else' in the general sense, no town, no souks, no entertainment, just one small hotel and a simple village, that one has more chance to touch the nature of the land and the people.

The Nefertari Hotel is small — it has just 30 rooms — pleasant, and rather reminiscent of safari hotels in East Africa. All the rooms have private bath and air conditioning, and it is rated three-star. I found the food quite good in a simple way; one does not expect gastronomic elaborations in the back of beyond. There is a swimming pool and tennis courts, and a comfortable bar. A new one-star hotel, the Ramesses, is scheduled.

Abu Simbel's History

Egypt is a country where man has always lived among things which are on a very large scale. Where life is divided between a great river and vast areas of desert. Perhaps that is why he had to build gargantuan monuments to hold his own with nature. At Abu Simbel you are on the edge of time, between the mastery of the desert and the Nile, now asserting itself as a lake.

One exciting thing to do is to take a taxi back to the temple area after dark and see the great façade by moonlight — if you happen to be there at a time near full moon. This lends a beauty and mystery to the mammoth statues which one cannot capture in the hard brilliance of sunlight.

For the rest, this is a place to relax in the great silence. At night there will be no sounds at all, except perhaps the eerie howling of a dog. The village where fisherfolk and farmers live, with the personnel of the airport, the custodians of the temples and a few other workers, goes to bed early. The visitor stays in a little island of modern life within the hotel.

What was it all like in the great remote world of the pharaohs, here about 1,200 kilometres (745 miles) from Memphis and the meeting point of Upper and Lower Egypt? The pharaohs of the Middle Kingdom conquered Nubia about 1900 BC. What of Nubia before that, and through all those generations till Ramesses II set his own particular seal on time here at Abu Simbel 600 years later?

Lake Nasser and Abu Simbel

We know that there were many temples all along the Nubian section of the Nile, and some are those which were salvaged in the great rescue operation of this generation, but of the people, the towns, the administration there seems to be very little known. How constant were the means of communication between first Memphis and later Thebes and these southerly outposts of empire? The river itself was the route, up from the mouth to the First Cataract where there was apparently a canal to bypass the rocks, and then again along the Nile.

There were viceroys and garrison towns, caravan posts and forts. Were there local governorates, the ancient equivalent of Egypt's modern system? How often did the pharaohs themselves make state visits to these places? Why did the mighty Ramesses choose this particular spot to create the largest and most extraordinary temples of all his temple-studded reign? They are comparable with the rock-cut wonders of Petra in Jordan, but those were carved 1,000 years later. It seems unlikely that these great focal points for worship and awe should have been set in a totally remote place. Perhaps Abu Simbel was a provincial capital, at a point where it was of particular importance that the Egyptian gods and the sacred status of the pharaohs themselves and their succeeding dynasties would be impressed upon the people. A people who had been conquered by the temporal power of those kings, who had also overcome the Libyan and Hyksos elements far away in Lower Egypt.

Much of what we know comes from those tomb inscriptions of the nobles at Aswan, perhaps still more will be discovered one day, or is known to specialists even now but somehow does not reach the ordinary reader or student. But in a way the flooding of the valley has sealed off both what is known and saved, and what more might have been discovered by excavation or inference from the lie of the land. That thought is tantalising, and yet perhaps the brief sojourner at Abu Simbel may be glad. It is a place to let the imagination have some rein.

Montazah Palace, Alexandria

Alexandria and The Nile Delta

If you look at a map of Egypt which shows the cultivated areas you will see an expanse of desert forming the background to a natural design like a long-stemmed rose. The stalk is the Nile, the flower being formed by the Delta with some detached leaves to the west provided by oases. This is in fact quite a good symbol for the country: the great river giving sap in the form of water, the rich fertile silt producing the blossom.

The Delta

More prosaically, the Delta is an irregular triangle spreading out from Cairo to the shores of the Mediterranean. Throughout its history this area of Lower Egypt has been the agriculturally productive region and therefore the main centre of population.

Alexandria and The Nile Delta

The Delta does not possess any centres of great architectural or historical interest. Some visitors may make the trip to the Nile Barrages, but for most it will only be seen when travelling from Cairo to Alexandria by certain routes. You can make the journey by train or by one of two main roads. The railway passes right through the fertile heart of the Delta, and so does one of the main roads. The other is the desert highway skirting the Delta to the west. By any of these routes — rail or road — the journey takes about two hours or a little more. If travelling by car it is a good plan to go one way by the Delta and to return by the desert route, on which you can visit the monasteries of Wadi Natrun, or vice versa.

Rail and dual carriageway road run quite close to each other for much of the way through this flat green world. There are many villages, the houses for the most part are the traditional brown mud brick ones, though new modern brick buildings are rising in various places. Small water channels dissect the fields, and there are moments when the scene is strangely reminiscent of southern France or even Normandy, apart from the people and the absence of most mechanical means of cultivation.

There are orchards with apple trees laden with ripe fruit at the end of March, fields of wheat, maize, onions and mint. Groups of date palms and eucalyptus trees with their grey-green, silvery leaves, bring back a more exotic touch. Look closer and it is Egypt indeed: a woman in a flowing reddish galebeah walks beside the road balancing a great basket on her head which is swathed in a handkerchief. There are water buffaloes the colour of Thames mud, and of course many donkeys. On the whole journey to Alexandria I only noticed one tractor though in fact there must have been many more, for modern methods are being gradually introduced. Still, for those who enjoy the sight of largely unchanged country life the Delta is a fascinating region and well worth a visit.

Two hallmarks of Egypt's immemorial rural life you will see in abundance. One is provided by the dovecotes or pigeon-houses. Pigeon is a very typical dish in Egypt and indeed throughout North Africa. Village and sometimes town dwellers have these large pigeoncotes beside their houses. They are mud built, round, pointed at the top and pierced with holes like a pepperpot, each hole having a small perch for the birds. You will find them all over Egypt, but in the well populated Delta one sees them continually.

The other typical sight is the primitive waterwheel where a blind-folded bullock walks round and round in a small circle harnessed to a pole which in turn rotates a big wooden cog-wheel. Attached to this is a series of pots which fill with water below ground level and then tip out automatically into a specially constructed channel above as the wheel brings them to the top of its revolution. A slow, laborious method of irrigation but one of the oldest, and still to be seen in most rural areas of Egypt.

Both road and rail go by way of Benha, one of the principal towns of the Delta, 44 kilometres (27 miles) from Cairo. Travelling by train (the 1st class is comfortable, air-conditioned and cheap, with a steward to bring you coffee and pastries in your pullman-type seats) one has little chance of assessing the character of Benha, except by means of a crowded platform of waiting passengers. Here, the eastern, or Damietta branch of the Nile is crossed.

Next comes Tanta, another important town almost in the centre of the Delta, and finally Damanhur some distance to the northwest and not far from Alexandria itself. In Damanhur the influence of the Mediterranean is already strong. Gone is the feeling of African mystery, remote culture or struggling traditional life. Damanhur is a smiling town with some handsome houses, two or three storeys high, with the picturesque green-painted shutters of southern Europe. There are gardens where roses bloom and bougainvillea spills its vivid pinkish-purple blossoms over walls and archways.

It is also possible to make the journey from Alexandria to Suez by bus; a method of transport which is surprisingly comfortable and enjoyable. The route is via Cairo, skirting the centre of the city, and the whole trip to Suez including the stop at Tanta takes five hours. The buses are air-conditioned coaches and the fares are low. The main difficulty is discovering the details of the available services, but the tourist office in Alexandria can supply information if you press for it and will also book your seat. It is advisable to get a ticket in advance: the bus, which runs daily, leaves from Alexandria's main bus station.

Alexandria

Egypt's second city, chief port and long-famous seaside resort is still passing through one of its transitional periods. There are people who bemoan the loss of its personality as a resort, its élan immortalised in Lawrence Durrell's *Alexandria Quartet.* That may well be true; I did not know the town when it was among the most famous of all places on the Mediterranean for the winter visitor, in the days when the European visitor sought not the blazing heat but gentle sunlit days. It was at that time that all the Riviera resorts burgeoned. On the whole, that atmosphere flourished best when there was a monarch who, with the court, made seasonal visits. The democratic outlook of Egypt's present-day Republic is quite foreign to the faded charm which Alexandria undoubtedly possessed. But the truth is that this experience was only a very short part of the city's long life. Alexandria's full history has been bold, brave and bloody.

Alexandria and The Nile Delta

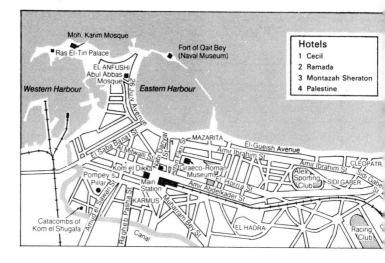

Alexander the Great

There was apparently an ancient Egyptian settlement here called Rhakotis, but the importance of the place did not, in fact, evolve gradually. The site was chosen by Alexander the Great in 332 BC. On his way to the Siwa Oasis, he chose this site to be the capital of his Empire because the island of Pharos protected it from western storms and made it potentially a fine naval base. He did not live to see his capital although his body was returned to the city after his death, for burial. In 316 BC, Ptolemy assumed power and founded the Ptolemaic Dynasty which lasted until the Roman conquest in 31 BC. The decline of the city began in the 3rd century AD and ended with its destruction by Diocletian.

In the early centuries of Christianity, Alexandria formed, with Rome and Constantinople, a great triumvirate of Christian faith and learning. Its streets were stained with the blood of St Mark and hundreds of other martyrs. Great Christian theologians of the early church spoke from Alexandria, and long before that in the 4th century BC, its university and library drew scholars from many lands. It became a centre for philosophers, poets and scientists.

Alexandria today

Today, one must look hard to find the memories of these ancient glories, but the position of the town is superb: it spreads along a series of bays where the blue Mediterranean comes in, capped with plumes of spray, sparkling in the sunshine. The corniche extends for some 25 kilometres (15 miles) east and west and behind this at varying points are the traditional Egyptian town, the administrative

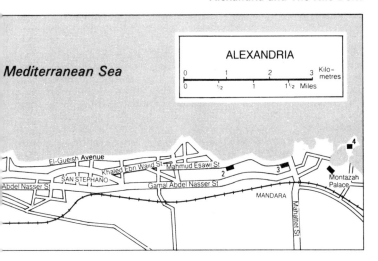

centre, the residential areas and, to the east, the palace and gardens of the former King Farouk, Montazah Palace.

Take Alexandria as it is. It is a place to enjoy in the present for its sea and beaches and lovely hot summer climate. Today it is essentially a summer resort, for the modern visitor demands much greater heat than did Europeans at the turn of the century. This is reflected in the prices: Alexandria's high season is from April to October, the exact opposite of the cities of Upper Egypt. In the spring and summer the residents of Cairo flock here to spend the day or weekend in cabins built on stilts along the corniche.

Pompey's Pillar

There is, however, a number of historical sites within the city area where different aspects of the past are partially revealed. One is known as Pompey's Pillar. In fact it had nothing to do with Pompey — the name was bestowed much later by the crusaders who believed that the ashes of Pompey had been placed in an urn on the platform at the top. This great column of red Aswan granite, more than 24 metres (80 feet) high, was built by a Roman prefect called Posthumus in honour of the Emperor Diocletian soon after AD 292.

At its foot and underground are the much older remains of the ancient temple of Serapis (the bull god): two long galleries cut out of the natural rock and faced with limestone. One has many niches in the walls, and one theory is that it was part of the temple library and the shelves were used to store rolls of papyrus. Other archaeolo-

115

gists believe it was used for the burial of sacred animals. The second gallery leads to a sanctuary designed for a statue of a god.

Above on the rough sandy hillocks, there are several sphinxes and statues, some Ptolemaic and some going back much farther, including a headless statue of Ramesses II. The pharaonic carvings were probably brought here from Heliopolis. Some of the most lively and colourful souks and street markets are in this area.

Catacombs
A few hundred yards to the south-west the non-Christian catacombs of Kom el-Shugafa extend to a depth of 30 metres (98 feet) and are arranged in three tiers of galleries, dating from the 1st and 2nd centuries AD. The visitor climbs down a circular staircase round a shaft by which the bodies were lowered for burial. There is much beautiful carving in the statues and cornices which show a fascinating blend of Graeco-Roman art and ancient Egyptian symbolism.

Pharos Island
On Pharos Island, which now forms the peninsula of Ras el Tin, was built the famous lighthouse which was hailed as one of the seven wonders of the world. Here was Cleopatra's palace and, beneath the soil of Alexandria, she and Antony are buried.

The lighthouse, which in its day was one of the tallest buildings in the world, was undermined and destroyed long ago, in early Arab times. It was rebuilt in the 10th century AD but was finally destroyed in the 14th century AD by an earthquake. The site is reputedly

Pompey's Pillar

covered by the 15th century Fort of Qait Bey which stands on the western arm of the East harbour. The three-storied fortified castle houses the Naval Museum while nearby are the Oceanographic Museum and the small Aquarium. The Pharos Island peninsula's northernmost tip is occupied by Ras el Tin Palace, a former residence of the royal family.

Abul Abbas Mosque
The principal mosque of Alexandria, that of Abul Abbas built in 1767, is on the tongue of land between the harbours in a district called El Anfushi. It is a magnificent building with four domes and a tall, delicate minaret like a carved ivory needlecase. Round the mosque is one of the typical old city areas.

In striking contrast are the big handsome squares and streets of tall buildings dating from the 19th and early 20th century when the government moved to Alexandria each summer and the city regained some of its ancient importance.

Kom el-Dikka Theatre
While foundations were being dug for a modern building, the Theatre of Kom el-Dikka, popularly known as the Roman Amphitheatre, was discovered only some 30 years ago. Twelve marble galleries form a semi-circle and it is the only example of this kind of theatre to have been found in Egypt. The original design and purpose however seems to have been changed several times between the 2nd and 6th centuries AD. Originally, it was a big auditorium about 40 metres (130 feet) wide, with 16 tiers of seats.

Later, this was modified, probably for use as an assembly hall for religious gatherings. There is a Roman bath in the same area where excavation work is still being carried out.

Most of these relics of the ancient city are in the area just behind the eastern harbour or between it and the western one. With a map and enough time to find your bearings by trial and error it is possible to visit many of them on foot, and often preferable to delays in traffic jams. In this respect, Alexandria is not so bad as Cairo, but quite bad enough to waste one's time and temper.

Graeco-Roman Museum
Most important of all, from the historical point of view is the Graeco-Roman Museum, which is considered second only to Cairo's great Antiquities Museum. Alexandria's museum is not very large, comprising a series of galleries built round two small gardens, but it contains a very fine collection founded some 90 years ago. Most of the exhibits are Ptolemaic and Roman and range from the 3rd century BC to the 3rd century AD. Many, but not all were found locally, some having been brought from places such as Fayoum. In the

gardens, tombs have been reconstructed and also a crocodile temple brought from Fayoum.

In the galleries there are inscriptions in Greek and Latin; tombstones, mummies, sarcophagi, mosaics, pottery, coins and jewellery, and two particularly striking examples of the mummy-portrait, painted with the wax technique known as 'encaustic' on a wooden panel and fastened over the head by the bands which swathe the mummy.

There are many fascinating things in this museum, from a startling bronze head of Hadrian with glass and ivory eyes to a collection of coloured glass which goes far back into the country's ancient culture. The Egyptians were the first people in the world to discover how to make glass, perhaps by accident, and their art of glazing has been traced from 4000 BC.

The Royal Jewellery Museum is also worth a visit, more, perhaps, for the building in which it is housed — the Fatima El-Zahraa Palace in Alexandria's Zezenia district — than for the exhibits. These are the family jewels of the 19th century Pasha Mohamed Ali.

There are other sights, but for most people this will probably be as much of the past as they want in Alexandria. Go eastwards along the seafront road, past the beaches and residential areas of Stanley Bay, San Stefano and Sidi Bisher, and eventually you will come to Montazah and the extreme eastern end of the city.

Montazah Palace

Here is a fairy-tale palace built by Khedive Abbas in 1892 which remained a royal residence until King Farouk's abdication in 1952. That time is apparently still too recent for Egyptians to talk readily about the King or indeed about his father King Fouad I, but the revolution and the republic have brought the Egyptian people into the domains of their former rulers. At present the Montazah Palace is closed for restoration but normally it is open as a museum.

The grounds, proudly walled and stretching along a beautiful section of coast extend for about 350 acres. The Palestine Hotel is within the park and as your taxi or car passes through the gates police check whether you are going there. Other visitors are charged 75 piastres per head to come into the park. Many come here, and where once an autocratic authority kept it all for private enjoyment now there are family groups sittings on the grass, playing, picnicking, walking, laughing and talking. Smiling teenagers stroll along the paths and ask you to photograph them; middle-aged couples walk sedately, and the sun sinks as impartially as it must have done before Alexander saw this as the setting for his own majestic city.

Hotels

There is a number of hotels in Alexandria of different grades, but not a great deal of choice for the discriminating visitor. Formerly the only five-star one was the Palestine Hotel which has 208 rooms and stands in a beautiful position on Montazah Bay. It is owned by the Egyptian Hotels Company and it is well run and comfortable. It is, however, some 10 kilometres (six miles) from the centre of Alexandria, and if you do not have transport this means taxis costing about LE 5 into town and back again.

Just outside the Montazah Park on the corniche road is the Montazah Sheraton, also five-star, more modern and luxurious than the Palestine, with 330 rooms; and in Sidi Bisher Bay (one bay nearer the city centre), is another five-star, the Ramada Renaissance, but the same problem of location applies to these also.

The four-star Cecil, now run by the Pullman Company in Saad Zaghlul Square is right in the heart of the town on the eastern harbour and close to the main railway and bus stations; noisy and crowded perhaps, but very well placed if you want to explore on foot. There are more than fifty other hotels, four-star and in the lower categories.

Restaurants
After Cairo, Alexandria is certainly the best equipped city in Egypt for eating out, though most of its restaurants are of the informal type. Santa Lucia is a good, fairly expensive restaurant in the centre of the town, and popular with tourists, tel. 4820372. Another is the Teka Grill, tel. 805119. Lord's Inn is also popular, tel. 5865664. Saraya's on the corniche is recommended, tel. 850884, as are Chez Gabi, tel. 4874406, and the seafood restaurant Seagull, tel. 4825575. The Elite (tel. 4823592) has a simple, genuine character and an excellent cuisine.

Sport
The Alexandria Sporting Club, the Smouha Club and the Yacht Club accept visitors as temporary members and provide facilities for golf, tennis and swimming, and there is horse racing in summer. The clubs have their own restaurants or cafeterias.

Abukir

Twenty-four kilometres (15 miles) east of Alexandria is the little port of Abukir, now also a seaside resort with the most sheltered beach on this section of the coast. The road there goes past the Montazah park and on over a level crossing. Trains seem to be fairly frequent on this local line, or perhaps I was simply unlucky. We had to wait for some time until the trains passed and gates opened. Meanwhile small boys did a brisk trade in polishing windscreens.

Abukir gained a name in European history when Nelson defeated

Alexandria and The Nile Delta

the French fleet in the bay here in 1798 — the famous Battle of the Nile. It also has roots far back in Egypt's history, for remains of a temple dedicated to Serapis and ancient public baths have been found, as well as traces of Napoleon's expedition a mere two centuries ago.

None of these things, however, form the real reason for going to Abukir, which has enough character of its own now to make more than one visit well worth while. It has three different faces: one is the little waterfront town, backed by wider modern streets. Leave the car off the main street and turn into this picturesque old quarter where narrow sandy tracks run down to the sea between the houses.

Puddles lie in these alleys and there is a fairly potent smell of fish mixed with drains. The houses are neither very old nor particularly attractive, and yet there is a vital, east Mediterranean quality, and genuine life. Children are playing, men tinkering with a car; washing flutters from lines stretched between the upper windows. In one street I watched three goats, four geese and four cats finding food in a large litter bin. Goats and geese wander freely everywhere in these alleys. From one small mosque a loudspeaker magnified the call to afternoon prayer until it seemed deafening in the narrow way. Beyond, in one of the metalled roads, a group of boys were playing football barefoot, their shoes serving as goalposts.

Perhaps half a mile away, one comes to the broad sheltered fishing beach. Gaily painted fishing boats are anchored or drawn up on the sand. Wooden tables and chairs are set at the edge of the water for the sale of fish. A fisherman with a peg-leg swings himself along over the hard sand; cars drive on the sands too, down to the water's edge and there are people, lots of them, busily coming to and from the boats. The distant houses, the light on the sea and the clarity of the air gives this scene a quaint affinity with a Breton fishing village.

But this is not all. The third face of Abukir is the little Egyptian resort where there is a much narrower sandy pleasure beach, deck chairs, coloured umbrellas, and rows of cars parked along the promenade. Across the road from the sea is the 'casino' which has nothing to do with gambling but is a place for refreshments. The town has one well-known fish restaurant, Zephyrion, which attracts gourmets from Alexandria.

Local Transport

Trains, buses and of course taxis or cars make Abukir an easy day or half-day excursion. If you stay long enough in Alexandria it is worthwhile sampling the local public transport. There are local buses and also trams which serve the different parts of this spreading city. Fares cost only a few piastres and for many visitors an Alexandrian tram is one of the highlights of the visit.

Lake Mareotis

Behind Alexandria and extending to the west is the Lake Mareotis area. Once this lake was much larger, but the western end is now just a shallow valley in the desert. In Alexander's time and long before and after the lake was large and famous, and its surroundings provided rich agricultural land. The ancients considered wine from the Mareotis region to be the best in Egypt. Devotees of Lawrence Durrell's novels will remember his description of the lake in the 1950s. 'Landscape tones: brown to bronze, steep skyline, low cloud, pearl ground with shadowed oyster and violet reflections ... Mareotis under a sky of hot lilac.'

Today the lake has shrunk and the city extended, but one can still see great areas of open water fringed with reeds and here and there a solitary fisherman in his boat. Just to the west of this there is an area of saltpans. In winter this is wet and slushy, but in summer it dries out and the salt shines white and sparkling like a magical ice field.

Modern day Nile boatman

Desert Oasis

The Western Desert

To the Egyptian, the Western Desert means the greater part of his country: the whole area west of the Nile Valley. All of it is arid desert except for a few scattered oases, the 'New Valley' and settlements west of Luxor. It is the beginning of the Sahara, which extends through Libya and westwards across the continent. To the European with a long memory, the phrase means that part of the North African coast and hinterland where the Eighth Army and Rommel's forces fought one of the great and decisive battles of the Second World War.

For the tourist the phrase is an evocative one for both these reasons, but the scope for exploration is extremely limited. Roads are almost non-existent, the desert vast, with few places to visit, and so for most people experience of the Western Desert will consist of driving from Cairo to Alexandria by the desert highway, and an excursion west along the coast to the battlefields and war cemeteries at El Alamein, possibly continuing to Mersa Matruh.

Alamein can be visited in a day excursion by car or coach trip from Alexandria. Mersa Matruh is rather too far for a day's outing, but there is a good beach hotel at Sidi Abdel Rahman a little way beyond Alamein.

West of Alexandria is the port area and the industrial section, but they can now be avoided by the new main roads.

A few minor roads lead off to small settlements in the desert to the south or to new developments on the coast, such as Sidi Kreir. The road follows the sea quite closely for most of the way, with glimpses of blue water over the sandhills. For Alamein, however, one continues westwards for 100 kilometres (63 miles) from Alexandria, over the yellowish-white stony desert with the sea always on the right-hand side. Much of this road is now built up with new towns and villages. The Maraqia Tourist Village lies just beyond Borg el-Arab, and farther on near Alamein an extensive ancient city of the Graeco-Roman period was discovered in 1985. It is known as the Marina Ruins, Alamein.

El Alamein

Nearly 50 years have passed since the Battle of Alamein was fought here. From October 23rd to November 4th 1942, the British Eighth Army under Montgomery fought a bitter battle against the Germans and Italians under Rommel in a successful bid to halt the advance of the North African corps. After the battle, in which over 11,000 soldiers of many nationalities were killed, the Allies assumed the offensive and advanced westwards to take Libya and Tunisia. Today, the thousands of lives that were lost are commemorated in the war cemeteries and memorials.

War Memorials
One comes first on the left-hand side of the road to a small memorial to the Greeks, who fell here on land where Greeks had ruled more than 2,000 years earlier. Then, again on the left, there is the British War Cemetery extending downwards into the valley.

The broad memorial cloister has simple, fine proportions and bears this inscription: 'Within this cloister are inscribed the names of soldiers and airmen of the British Commonwealth and Empire who died fighting on land or in the air where two continents meet and to whom the fortune of war denied a known and honoured grave, with their fellows who rest in this cemetery, with their comrades in arms of the Royal Navy and with the seamen of the Merchant Navy, they preserved for the West the link with the East and turned the tide of war'. In the pavement is a central stone with the words 'To the Glory of God and to the undying memory of the Eighth Army, 23rd October-4th November, 1942.

It is very quiet in the shade of the cloister where the memorial books record the names of those who died. More than half came from the United Kingdom but there were many from India and Pakistan, others from South Africa, Australia, New Zealand, Canada, East Africa, West Africa and the Sudan, as well as Frenchmen and Poles.

The Western Desert

Beyond are the rows of gravestones, each the same shape and size, erected with military precision, but each with its own inscription and all beautifully maintained. At the far end, with the desert stretching away into the distance, stands a great stone cross with a sword superimposed on it, the point downwards.

There is a very moving union of the general and the particular here. In one place Egypt pays her own tribute: 'The land on which this cemetery stands is the gift of the Egyptian people for the perpetual resting place of the sailors, soldiers and airmen who are honoured here'. Spare a little time to walk among the graves themselves. Some stones, clearly the graves of unidentified bodies, simply bear the words 'Known to God'.

Further along the road at Tell el-Eisa, a 12 kilometres (7½ mile) distance which separates the memorials of those who in their fighting lives were enemies, are the graves of the Italian and German soldiers. The German memorial is well away from the road, you have to drive over a rough winding track to reach it. Here, there is a great octagonal monument, built of golden stone, which rises starkly from the desert and which contains the ashes of the known dead. Inside, a central obelisk is surrounded by memorial arcades with bronze tablets where individual names are listed. Great tomb-like monuments represent the different German regions. There is also a grave of 31 unknown soldiers, whose nationality and allegiance could not be determined, and which is marked with the simple inscription: 'Death knows no country'.

Do not miss the German memorial. Inside a few birds wheel above the sunlit courtyard. There is a compelling dignity about the place and it is an essential part of Alamein, its silence of a different quality from that of the British acres.

Finally, one comes to the Italian memorial which is different again: open, sunlit, close to the roadside, a place of stone cloisters, flowers and a small museum.

Military Museum

In the village of El Alamein itself is the Military Museum and what is rather cryptically described as the Spoils Exhibition. There are, of course, weapons, tanks, guns, parachutes and much of the general equipment used by both the Allies and the Axis forces in the North African campaign of 1942. They are genuine, and very interesting to any student of recent military history. And there are maps and reliefs and a great deal to clothe the bare facts and dates with meaning. All the military commanders and personalities of that time in the war — Montgomery, Rommel, Graziano — are depicted here in flamboyant paintings.

The museum is worth a visit, and not least because it now includes a section of Egypt's own '10th of Ramadan, 6th October, 1973', the war in which she regained the Suez Canal.

There is a small resthouse and cafeteria beside the museum, but there is no very comfortable place to linger in Alamein. One comes here as a form of pilgrimage, personal or historical. Leave it with a sense of the majesty of the desert and the dead. It is probably best to bring a packed lunch, unless you are going straight on to Sidi Abdel Rahman. There are still some unexploded mines in the area so it is advisable to keep to the main road when walking.

Sidi Abdel Rahman

There are few problems in finding the right road in Egypt for, except in towns, there is seldom any choice — local, minor roads being little more than tracks. Follow the westward road, then, from El Alamein and in another 20 kilometres (12 miles) or so you will come to the turning point to Sidi Abdel Rahman.

The beach hotel is visible from the main road as a group of low white buildings away across the sands to the right, and the side road leads there in a few minutes. There is a small village at Sidi Abdel Rahman though no one remembers to mention it: the name comes from the mosque which is a shrine of Abdel Rahman, a saintly man who was especially venerated by the Bedouin. For the visitor, however, this is simply a place for beach relaxation, and very delightful it is, with clean sparkling water and brilliant white sand.

The hotel is actually called the El Alamein Hotel but everyone speaks of it as Sidi Abdel Rahman. It is an attractive place, built right on the edge of the beach in a calm, Mediterranean bay. The hotel is rated four-star and has 99 rooms as well as villas. The public rooms are spacious, the pale gold sands inviting. Something of a garden has been created here in the desert, and there are trees and grass and some brilliant flowers.

This hotel, now run by the Pullman Company, is popular with well-to-do Egyptians for family holidays. For the tourist it is a pleasant place to relax for a few days in the midst of the strenuous tour, or to stay for a night or two while exploring both Alamein and Mersa Matruh. Two points should be borne in mind. One, that it is essential to book well in advance; to arrive hoping to be accommodated is to court disaster for there is nowhere else to stay. Secondly the hotel is seasonal, and open from April to October only, though in the future they hope to stay open throughout the year.

Beyond the Sidi Abdel Rahman turning the western road continues over open desert with few signs of life. It is now a good road, dual carriageway for most of the 290 kilometres (181 miles) from Alexandria to Mersa Matruh. By car the drive takes 3½ hours. There are also bus and train services.

Mersa Matruh

This little port has character, a long history, and one of the most beautiful beaches on the Mediterranean with seven kilometres (four miles) of soft, silvery white sand. Colour is everywhere — the incredible turquoise and sapphire of the sea rivals that of the Arabian Gulf. There are brilliant umbrellas on the beach and the local form of tourist transport consists of little donkey carriages, also with colourful awnings. The Siwa Museum which mirrors Bedouin life in the famous Siwa Oasis is well worth a visit.

In the days of the Ptolemies and the Romans it was the western cornerstone of Egyptian defences; they called it Paraetonium then. Cleopatra built palaces here, but even earlier it was an important port and trading centre en route to the temple of Amun at Siwa.

The town is on a lagoon sheltered from the sea by a chain of rocks and west of the main harbour, beyond a large rock, is a special lagoon known as Cleopatra's Bath where according to tradition the Ptolemaic queen bathed during her visits. It can be reached by walking a couple of kilometres along the shore or by sailing boat.

On the eastern edge of the town is Rommel's Cave, where the German commander drew up his battle plans for Tobruk. It is now a museum containing personal relics, maps and clothing. Presented by Rommel's son, it is well maintained, dignified and moving.

Hotels

There are now some 15 hotels of most grades. The new Miami Hotel with more than 200 rooms was not yet graded at the time of my visit, but should rate four-star. It overlooks the sea and is well equipped. In the three-star category there are several, among them the Attic, Negresco and Beau Site; the latter was one of the first hotels here and caters for individual travellers, not groups. For a very inexpensive, ungraded, hotel the Adriatica is quite adequate.

West of Mersa Matruh

Westwards there are some beautiful beaches, notably Ageeba, 28 kilometres (17 miles) from Matruh, which is scenically very striking with cliffs and caves. It is reached by a secondary coast road passing through fig and olive orchards parallel with the sea, glimpsed through white sand dunes. On the way you pass through Qasr where Cleopatra's palace is believed to have stood, then Abyad with a lovely beach, and then another village, Om Rakham, where there are the remains of a Ramesses II temple.

The road continues for another 225 kilometres (140 miles) west from Matruh to Sallum on the Libyan border. The whole situation here was changed by the opening of the Egyptian-Libyan frontier in spring 1990. There are even bus services from Alexandria into Libya.

Oases

Siwa, 330 kilometres (206 miles) south of Mersa Matruh, is the historic oasis to which Alexander the Great went to consult the oracle at the Temple of Amun, choosing the site for the foundation of Alexandria on the way. In the past few years the Siwa Oasis has also become accessible to the ordinary visitor, where once it involved something of an expedition. It lies 20 metres (65 feet) below sea level and has a population of 6,000, most of whom live in the village of Aghurmi. The people are mainly Berber and Bedouin and because of their isolation have retained much of their culture and traditions. Their handicrafts and products, such as dates and olive oil, are sold in Mersa Matruh.

It is still necessary to have a special permit before travelling to the oasis, but this is readily available through the Matruh Tourist Office. Which can supply information about Siwa accommodation. There are regular bus services Matruh-Siwa.

To the east of Siwa lies the Qattara Depression, a large area which is 133 metres (436 feet) below sea level.

Much farther south there are other oases of the Western Desert: Farafra (reached from Cairo), Dakhla, and El Kharga with roads from Asyut. These last are about the same latitude as Luxor, but none is really feasible to visit for the ordinary holiday-maker.

Suez Canal Authority Building, Port Said

Suez and the Canal

The strip of country which since 1869 has been cut by the Suez Canal was from time immemorial the land link between Africa and Arabia. Potentates and armies, pilgrims and merchants travelled across it, the one great bridge between north and south. In modern times the Canal has provided an even more important sea link between west and east. This area of Suez, known in biblical times as Goshen, is by every standard historic ground.

As such, it is a region which any visitor who is interested in more than the pharaonic heritage of Egypt should try to see. Comparatively few do, though it is quite easy for anyone who has a day or two to spare.

There are regular train services from Cairo to Ismailia and Port Said, with connections to Suez, and even a few from Alexandria. There is a good road and it is only 134 kilometres (84 miles) to Suez. The regular bus service is in air-conditioned coaches, comfortable, cheap and taking less than two hours, departing from the

Cairo coach station. It would be quite possible to go there for a day from the capital.

Suez

On arrival one finds Suez in a state of rehabilitation. It was virtually destroyed in the Egyptian — Israeli war of 1973 after which Egypt regained control of the Canal under a negotiated settlement. The Israelis had taken the Sinai peninsula in the 1967 war and dug in along the east bank. For the eight years from then until 1975, the Canal was closed. During that time normal life virtually died in the Egyptian towns to the west: the trade of the seaway and the land transit connection ceased, and many people left to find work elsewhere.

Since 1975 however, life has come back and Suez, though still battle scarred, is busy rebuilding. There is a sharp division between Port Tewfik at the southern entrance of the Canal, handsomely rebuilt, and the town of Suez on its bay. Between the two, a matter of two or three kilometres (1½ miles), is the broad dual carriageway road from the main town to Port Tewfik along the side of the bay.

I have walked it several times, once adopted by a giggling posse of schoolgirls eager to improve their English, who suddenly fled to catch a bus to their home districts. One makes many unexpected acquaintances in Egypt, especially in places where few tourists penetrate.

The heart of Suez is a sprawling network of shabby streets and souks just behind the bay, and behind that again lies the new town where big blocks of rather handsome flats are being built with their own shopping areas and schools.

It is fashionable to dismiss Suez as characterless and uninteresting. I like it. I enjoy its unpretentious realism, its pride in struggling back to a worthwhile life, even its cheeky little boys who follow you about on foot or on bicycles.

The souks of Suez are well worth exploring — for a sight of the local life rather than for one's own shopping, since they do not cater for tourists. Choose late afternoon as the sun is going down, and then walk back to Port Tewfik where you will probably be staying, as the better hotels are there.

At sundown, the bay of Suez is strangely beautiful and evocative in its own way. The water is brilliantly blue while the sun is up, and there are great patches of bright green weed and gaily coloured fishing boats. Then the light changes and the whole becomes a study in grey and black, with sharp outlines and bars of apricot and lemon across the sky and reflected on the dark water. Ships wait in the bay before they pass through the Canal in the northern direction, and I counted 30 of them one evening, large and small, with their lights twinkling through the shadows.

Port Tewfik

Much money and effort must have been spent in restoring Port Tewfik. There are attractive gardens beside the Canal, one of the presidential official residences, some pleasant residential roads and two reasonably good hotels. You can take an hour's boat trip round the entrance to the Canal and see the waiting ships.

Passengers travelling westwards who leave their ships in order to visit Cairo during the Canal transition disembark here, and rejoin their vessel at Port Said. There are also some regular Red Sea cruises which go across to the Gulf of Aqaba and neighbouring waters and do not pass through the Canal. Passengers and crew often have a night or two to spend at Suez, hence the hotels in Port Tewfik.

Hotels

The best-known hotel is the rebuilt Summer Palace, which is on the bay in Port Tewfik but facing away from the port itself and the entrance to the Canal. It is rated three-star, has 77 twin-bedded rooms, and there are facilities for sailing, water ski-ing and surfing. It is a restful, attractive place to stay.

One or two streets away on the other side of Port Tewfik is the newer Red Sea Hotel. This is three-star with 28 well-equipped modern rooms and pleasant staff, eager to please.

There are two two-star hotels in Suez itself. The Beau Rivage is now called a hotel-motel. It was simple but friendly when I last stayed there, and the cooking was good. The other two-star establishment is the White House.

The Canal

A waterway link between the Mediterranean and the Red Sea was by no means an idea of the 19th century, but the ancient system utilised the Nile for the north-western section. The first channels were cut about 2100 BC: some 200 years later another was constructed between the Red Sea and Bitter Lakes and the Nile, and known as the Canal of the Pharaohs. This was apparently in use for 1,000 years. Much later, in the 6th century BC it was re-dug and operated once more. It was extended to the Mediterranean by Ptolemy II and used well into the Roman period. In AD 98 the Emperor Trajan had its course altered to join the Nile near the site of modern Cairo to improve trade routes. It was again neglected, although records show that it was used by the Arabs as late as the 8th century.

Napoleon saw the importance of a sea route here to India and the Far East, but the project came to nothing because Napoleon's engineer, due to a wrong calculation, declared the level of the Red Sea to be 10 metres (33 feet) higher than that of the Mediterranean and the work therefore not practicable.

Mention of de Lesseps and his own triumph with the Suez Canal and its later place in the traumas of Middle East history has been made in the historical chapter of this book. Today the canal is in full operation again, widened and deepened to take larger ships.

The canal is 171 kilometres (107 miles) long (two and a half times the length of the Panama Canal) and the third longest canal in the world. It passes through Lake Timsah, the Great Bitter Lake and Little Bitter Lake between Ismailia and Suez. It is 140 metres (459 feet) wide. There is a very sophisticated navigation system operated by the Traffic Offices in Ismailia, Port Said and Suez, and 11 guiding stations along the canal with radar network and radio transmission centres. Over 20,000 ships pass through the canal each year, which was nationalised by the Egyptian Government in 1956.

All the same it still appears an amazingly narrow channel to carry so much of the world's vital transport, and for that reason is all the more fascinating.

Along the Canal
With a car it is easy to drive along the west side to Ismailia and on to Port Said. I made a day trip from Suez to Ismailia by local transport, and can thoroughly recommend this for anyone who wants to see the area from the inside, as it were, and at minimal cost.

I started by taking a seat in a 'service taxi' at Suez bus station. This cost me LE 2 (probably rather more now) for the one-way journey. We waited about 10 minutes until the taxi filled up with other passengers: a young man with his mother and three other youngish men all of whom were courteous and friendly, and anxious to talk in English, exchange names and addresses and hear about the book I was writing.

We took a road leading north from Suez and over the desert, well out of sight of the Canal. As we came nearer to Ismailia we came into a rich agricultural region, very green, with villages of mud brick houses grouped under palm trees. The locals were working in the fields, riding donkeys or gravely watching our taxi as we delivered first one and then another of our passengers to their homes. There were a lot of the pepperpot pigeoncotes here as in the Delta. The trip took about an hour.

For the return journey I took the local bus from Ismailia which is even cheaper. As we sat in the bus at the bus station, boys got on selling bread, sweetmeats and cans of coca-cola. Outside a shoe-black was plying his trade while over the bus radio came the evocative, unexpected music of Wagner's 'Ride of the Valkyries'.

With the bus we took a different route, which was remarkably beautiful and exciting. First along the side of the Canal itself and then round the shore of the Great Bitter Lake. Up the channel came the stately procession of ships, bearing names and countries of origin on bow and stern. There were Jugoslav, Cuban, Greek, British vessels and a dozen more. On the broader waters of the lake were fishing boats and some small sailing yachts. From its shores fishermen walked home carrying their nets over their shoulders.

Finally we turned inland to the desert again for the last few kilometres into Suez. The two journeys together had cost me less than one pound sterling, or two dollars, and I had had an insight into a living part of Egypt totally unknown to most tourist visitors.

Ismailia

Completely unlike Suez, Ismailia has a character which is I think best described as gracious. I have been told that it was quite as war-torn as Suez, and yet it has revived in a way which has retained much of the mood of the 19th century while being very busy in bringing the Canal Zone into the picture of life in modern Egypt.

The town stands midway along the Canal and has no ancient foundations. It was built by de Lesseps as a base for the Suez Canal Company, and it stands on the western shore of Lake Timsah (the Crocodile Lake) which lies some distance north of the Great Bitter Lake, both being part of the Suez Canal route. Originally the settlement was called El Timsah Village when it was founded in 1863 but was later renamed Ismailia in honour of the Khedive Ismail, Egypt's ruler at that time.

Gardens are the hallmark of Ismailia; large, long-established public gardens with great trees, flowering shrubs, water channels, and a leisurely, old-world mood of well-being. There are tree-lined boulevards, and large, handsome public buildings. But if the inhabitants are proud to regard it as a garden city it is also a cultural one. Being in the centre of the Canal Zone the Suez Canal University has its main campus here, with faculties of agriculture, science, education and medicine. Other branches of the same university are in Port Said, and at Suez, which accommodates the petroleum and mining sections.

These three cities work as a triumvirate, each being a governorate in its own right, but Suez and Port Said are city areas, while the Ismailia governorate includes the surrounding country up to the urban boundaries of the other two. Eighty per cent of the university students, two-fifths of whom are women, are drawn from the Canal area and also Sinai.

There are few actual 'sights' in Ismailia. The principal ones are the Ismailia Museum, the de Lesseps Museum, the Suez Canal Authority's Research Centre and, above all, the Canal itself. Still there are other things, among them the Al-Shafer Mosque beside the Canal which is not architecturally outstanding itself but is near the presidential residence. The juxtaposition of another place of worship gives it a special character too. Across the narrow street leading down to the water is a small Roman Catholic church which, I was told, was built by a French doctor who went there to pray before performing operations at the nearby hospital.

Hotels

So far Ismailia has not become a holiday resort, and it has all the more character for that reason, but tourism is one of the many avenues which the remarkably active local administration means to open up.

In the meantime the accommodation for the visitor is perfectly adequate. There is the charming four-star Etap Ismailia Hotel on Forsan Island with 152 rooms, and the El Morsan Village, also four-star, four two-star and two one-star hotels.

Express trains from Cairo to Ismailia take two-and-a-half hours. As with Suez it is a short journey by road — 120 kilometres (75 miles) — and there are good bus services.

Port Said

Up at the northern end of the Canal, Port Said has long had a reputation all its own. Even among the world's other well-known seaports Port Said has, for more than a century, been familiar to travellers and mildly notorious to those for whom the glamour of the East is filtered through books and the experiences of others.

Perhaps sadly, this aspect of its life as a port of call for liners has gone, because there are virtually no long-distance liners today. In 1990 I was told that the *Canberra* comes through the Canal once a year and calls at Port Said, and she is the only one. But local, east

Suez and the Canal

Mediterranean cruise ships call weekly. It also remains an important centre for shipbuilding and repair – this part of its life being centred in the dock area at Port Fouard on the opposite, east bank of the Canal – as well as being Egypt's second port and a free trade centre. More recently it has become a seaside resort, very popular with Egyptians.

The modern city dates from 1859 and came into being with the Canal, but its history can be traced back to pharaonic times when it was called Pelusium, and the estates of Amun here included rich orchards and vineyards. The Ptolemies called it Al-Farma and it was known by that name into the Christian era. Tradition holds that the Holy Family made their flight into Egypt through Al-Farma. Later the records of the Arab conquest of the country name it as one of the first towns to be captured.

There is a diversity of things to see. The Port Said National Museum is a splendid modern one with many treasures well displayed. The rooms devoted to the Coptic and Islamic periods are particularly interesting. There are 'landmarks' such as the Suez Canal Authority Building and the Custom House. The de Lesseps statue was banished from the quayside in 1956, and it is a matter of debate whether it be returned to its plinth or kept in the museum. Boat trips among the shipping here at the head of the Suez Canal are fascinating. On one restaurant boat (owned by the Noras Tourist Village) you can eat quite well while you circle the big ships.

The town has two well-known mosques, those of Abdel Rahman and El Abbas, the Coptic church of Mari Gergis, the Catholic Cathedral and the Military Museum.

Hotels

The El Noras Tourist Village at the heart of Port Said and with a fine beach is the newest development, and will probably rate four-star. It has self-contained units, swimming pools, restaurants, shops, facilities for children, and is immensely popular for family holidays. There is also the pleasant four-star Helnan Port Said Hotel (formerly ETAP); the New Regent, Holiday and Palace Hotels, all three-star; and a number of two- and one-star hotels.

A charge is made on the road when entering and leaving the free trade zone of Port Said. For private cars this is LE1 in each direction.

St Anthony's Monastery

Red Sea Coast and Sinai

The Red Sea thrusts a two-pronged fork into the great bridge of land between north-east Africa and Arabia. The eastern prong is the Gulf of Aqaba with Saudi Arabia along its further shore and, at the farthest extremity, a short length of Jordanian coast and that country's one seaport Aqaba, facing a section of Israeli territory and their town of Eilat. The western prong is the Gulf of Suez with the entrance to the Canal at the top.

Between the two is the broad Sinai peninsula. Now that that region has been restored to Egypt she has a great deal of coastline; not only on both sides of the Gulf of Suez but southwards all along the Red Sea shore, into the level of the tropics. In this chapter we shall look first at the Egyptian African Coast.

Beyond the Tropic of Cancer (which crosses Egypt just south of Aswan) lies a world perhaps better known to the ancients than to most people today. Away to the south was the land of Punt, believed to be the Somalia of today, and the Horn of Africa, but north of it is Egypt all the way.

Red Sea Coast and Sinai

Vast expanses of desert and mountain lie behind this shore; most of the fertility is in the sea, for the Red Sea is rich in fish. Until very recently, these great stretches of beach have been part of the waste lands of Egypt, but with the country's development into a modern world which has a large, sun-starved, sea-loving population, a sizeable proportion of whom have leisure and means to travel, Egypt has begun to create holiday resorts here.

The setting is quite different from that of Egypt's Mediterranean littoral. There she must compete with all the other Mediterranean countries, many of which have more to offer the western visitor. The Red Sea shore of Egypt has a remote, primeval character. There are unlimited sands, warm sea and virtually nothing else. It is another world from the archaeological heritage of the Nile, though the two can be combined by holidaymakers. How far and how successfully this area can become an economically productive region in the tourist industry remains to be seen.

An enormous amount will have to be done to create the infrastructure of roads and services, accommodation and even entertainment required by mass tourism. At present the visitor must be content with simplicity and to a great extent solitude except in the actual places where they stay. But that is the magic of it. Go to the Red Sea now, and at least for a few more years to come, and you will be as near the basic elements of inanimate nature as one is likely to be within a few hours of civilisation.

Routes to Hurghada

Hurghada was the first resort to be developed on the western Red Sea coast. There are several ways of getting there. EgyptAir has two flights daily to and from Cairo which take 60 minutes. Planes land on a local airstrip a few kilometres from the town of Hurghada and close to the two tourist venues, the Sheraton Hotel and the Magawish Tourist Village. Air Sinai also has twice weekly flights from Cairo, one linking with Sharm El Sheikh. There are daily buses from Cairo and, I believe, a service from Luxor.

Or you may drive from Cairo (see below). The distance is 529 kilometres (329 miles) and for most of the way the road follows the coast. You can also drive from Luxor, a distance of 290 kilometres (180 miles).

It was this last route that I took, and for anyone who enjoys desert scenery it is wholeheartedly recommended. For the first part of the journey, which takes about an hour, you follow the Nile Valley from Luxor down to Qena; a road which passes through the living world of the Nile villages, their people, animals and crops; a slow-moving panorama of the life bestowed by the great river, green and gentle under the power of the sun.

At Qena you branch off north-eastwards and almost immediately are in the desert. There is a direct road to Hurghada but it is not such a good one. My driver took the main road which runs for 160 kilometres (99 miles) to the Red Sea port of Safaga and then up the coast about another 50 kilometres (31 miles) to Hurghada.

Part of it is flat, interminable sandy desert, but there are hills and lesser mountains, gold and brown, rugged and seamed with small wadis. Above, the sky is immeasurably high, pale blue and the sun casts sharp shadows in the hills. There are no towns, no villages, just a road which winds on and on among the gorges, eastwards into the unknown, at least for the first-time traveller.

A certain amount of traffic passes up and down this road; trucks and rather battered Egyptian cars full of cheerful, smiling people with luggage piled precariously high on the roofs.

At one point there was a desert 'pull-in for cabmen' where the drivers of several heavy trucks had congregated and were eating and drinking. With grave courtesy I and my driver were brought little cups of coffee and I sat on the small verandah smoking and exchanging a few words with a young army officer and two or three of his men while my driver changed wheels.

On and on again through the hills with, here and there, a hawk hovering. Where does he find the life on which to swoop? At last blue water under the blue sky, and we were in sight of the sea.

Safaga

Safaga is quite a busy port. I saw little of it except warehouses and factories and oil tanks, and the area of small shack-like dwellings near the port. There is, however, a resort hotel here: the two-star Safaga Hotel (30 rooms) which is under the same management as the Summer Palace at Suez. It is a modern well-equipped beach hotel. There are camping facilities at the waterfront and a German-managed diving base: diving, windsurfing, sailing and fishing are the chief attractions here as at Hurghada.

This coast is one of the tourist development areas. Eighty kilometres farther south there are camping sites at Al Qusseir, and 135 kilometres beyond that are rest houses at Marsa Alam, famous as a fishing centre.

Hurghada

This is one of the most striking examples of a place which has developed a split personality through tourism. Hurghada is a smallish, straggling, unlovely town on the coast, sheltered by a headland of sandy cliffs to the south. But it is alive, a place where people live and work. The streets of souks are wide, the shops open-fronted as elsewhere and they meet the local demands. Here are the ubiquitous bales of cloth (a lot of material is used for the flowing veils and galebeahs); there a man is being shaved while the barber carries on a conversation not only with his customer but with passers-by. Fruit and vegetables, spices and meat are displayed, and always quantities of plastic things, from pails and bottles to flowers and children's sandals. And there are several of those cafés where quiet men of varying ages sit playing dominoes, or talk across a table bearing a single empty coffee cup. The atmosphere of these cafés always seems meditative rather than convivial.

I walked through these souks and on by dusty streets, past the telegraph office and so to the centre of the new Hurghada. For the town has clearly taken on a recent dignity and importance since the re-opening of the Suez Canal. There are some large and impressive new buildings, including a very beautiful modern mosque. New, wide roads have been built. Hurghada is the administrative centre of a large governorate. It has a Marine Life Museum and Aquarium visited by most of the tourists who come here.

There is a road bordering the sea at Hurghada though it hardly qualifies for the popular title of corniche. The souks and offices lie well away behind this, but the mosque is near the sea and after walking past it I came to the southern end of this seaside road and found that some rather handsome private bungalows have been built there, on the edge of the steep beach. Flowers gave them a leisured grace. At the road end of a small path leading down to the sea between them was a notice board with the words 'Please put on your clothes before leaving the shore (avoid penalty)'. It was written in English and French.

That reveals the split personality of resorts like these. Hurghada is growing in importance as an Egyptian provincial town, very remote from the regular areas of ancient culture and modern development; but what now makes its name known in many parts of the world through travel agents' brochures is that it is developing as a tourist resort. Moreover its particular breed of tourist is the sun-and-sea one who is much farther removed from the traditional Egyptian way of life and thinking than is the culture vulture who follows the pharaohs.

Hotels
In the bay of Abu Menka five kilometres (three miles) to the south, both the Sheraton Hotel and the Magawish Tourist Village are situated. I found the five-star Hurghada Sheraton (85 rooms) a delightful hotel in most respects. It is a circular building built round an open patio bar. The bedrooms with their balconies and dining

room look out over the sea. There is a particularly attractive terrace with a swimming pool surrounded by artificial grass — it is extraordinary how much visual pleasure this green gives in a brilliant world of sun and sand and shining sea. The food is quite good, and the service courteous and most helpful, though the dining room is very crowded in the evenings. The majority of people staying here are groups from international diving clubs, as the hotel has full facilities for scuba diving, fishing and so on. It is this beach about which I have some reservations. The sand is mixed with small sharp stones and there are patches of slimy mud: but for sun-bathing it is delightful, with plenty of lounge chairs and thatched 'umbrellas' for shelter. A hotel bus takes visitors to and from the town of Hurghada several times a day.

Tourist Village
Three kilometres (two miles) along the beach at the southern end of the bay is Magawish Tourist Village. Here the whole concept is entirely different from the hotel amenities of the Sheraton. Hurghada is considered the best place for underwater fishing on this Red Sea coast. The sea bed slopes gently downwards in this bay and in the middle there is a huge coral formation. The area is sheltered from desert winds from the west and the sea is virtually free from strong currents and undertows. Hence its choice as a resort area. The tourist village is run by the Egyptian government-owned travel agency Misr Travel.

It takes its style entirely from Club Mediterranée who formerly operated it, and is comparable to their seaside villages in many other countries. There are 204 stone built, twin-bedded chalets scattered along the beach. There is a large restaurant seating 600 and the food is good, as one would expect with the French influence.

Obviously the real raison d'être of the place is its well-equipped diving centre, sailing school and motor boats available for sea trips and fishing, but there are other sports: tennis and table tennis, basket ball, volley ball and archery.

The village is rated four-star and charges include not only accommodation and meals but all the main sports facilities available.

There is now another four-star tourist village, El Mashrabiya, the three-star El Gifton Tourist Village, also the three-star El Gezirah Tourist Hotel and the Princess Club.

Road from Hurghada to Cairo
As indicated, this is a very long drive, and entails going all along the Red Sea coast to Suez and taking the Cairo road there. Almost halfway along the coast section you come to Ras Gharib, now a thriving town because of oil wells in the neighbourhood. North of

here, near Ein Sukhna which is about 60 kilometres (37 miles) from Suez are two more famous old Coptic monasteries, those of St Paul and St Anthony. They can be reached by car, and permission to visit them must be obtained from the office of the Coptic Patriarch in Cairo (see General Information).

Sinai

This historic, almost wholly desert peninsula was restored to Egyptian sovereignty in 1979. The northern section is sandy plain; in the centre lies hilly country where gazelles survive in the wild; to the south rise great mountains, austere, magnificent and cruel to the traveller of old. In winter the heights are snow-covered.

In 1982 a two-lane road tunnel was opened. It passes under the Canal 17 kilometres (10 miles) north of Suez and has changed the whole pattern of access to Sinai. Never a region where agriculture could exist except in very small areas, Sinai is rich in minerals such as oil and magnesium. Its oil fields now produce more than three-quarters of Egypt's oil production. The history of mining in Sinai goes back to the ancient Egyptians. There were turquoise, magnesium and iron mines in the southern part of the peninsula, and there are traces of oil on the land surface in some areas. Tar may have been transported from here for use in mummification.

Right through history this area has been linked with Egyptian religious beliefs. It was in Sinai that Isis was supposed to have sought the dismembered body of murdered Osiris. The goddess of love and fertility, Hathor, was associated with it, and pharaohs called her Our Lady of Sinai.

For the three great monotheist religions it was the place where Moses received the ten commandments from God, and Christians and Moslems recognise it as the land crossed by Mary and Joseph with the infant Jesus as they fled from Herod.

St Catherine Monastery

Many early Christians went to Sinai to escape their Roman persecutors, and the famous St Catherine Monastery was founded in the 6th century on the traditional site of the burning bush on the slopes of Mt Sinai. It stands right in the centre of the southern half of Sinai and is dedicated to St Catherine of Alexandria, a young Christian virgin who, subjected to many kinds of torture, would not yield her faith, but instead converted those who were sent to interrogate her, including the wife of the Emperor Maximinius (AD 305–313). At last the infuriated emperor ordered Catherine to be tied to a spiked wheel which would tear her body to pieces (from this we have the catherine-wheel), but she was miraculously delivered from that and eventually beheaded by the emperor's command in AD 307.

The monastery is Greek Orthodox (not Coptic) and is built like a mediaeval fortress in the mountains. It has a world famous library of rare manuscripts and books, with more than 2,000 Hellenic manuscripts, hundreds of Latin and Arabic ones, and others of different cultures, Coptic, Ethiopian, Polish, English, French, Armenian. Some go back well before the building of the monastery, and the most famous of all is the 4th century Codex Sinaiticus, which has been called the most famous biblical manuscript in the world. It contains the whole of the New Testament, part of the Old Testament and two non-canonical works.

The monastery includes the ancient church with its stained glass and icons, the library, an olive press, a wine press, store houses, two windmills, kitchen, ovens, a house for the bishop and the guests, accommodation for the monks (there are now twenty of them) and a refectory. There is a garden where figs, grapes, walnuts, quince, mulberries, olives and other fruit and nuts are grown, as well as vegetables, and the birds sing gently in the trees beside the stream.

No description can convey the beauty and remoteness of the St Catherine Monastery high up among peaks which rise to 2,285 metres: sun-bleached, red gold mountains.

The monastery is open from 0900 till 1200 daily except Fridays and Sundays. There is no entrance charge, and visitors are not even asked for alms. The ordinary visitor sees the main church, the Burning Bush Chapel and surroundings. To visit the library and some other parts not usually open to visitors advance application must be made to the Greek Orthodox office at 18 el Zaher in Cairo; tel. 828 513.

Tourist Village

A new and handsome tourist village has been opened in the valley below. It has 100 air-conditioned granite bungalows and a fine restaurant building which serves ample if not very elegant meals. It is graded four-star and is good value. No alcohol is available, a rule of the monks. There is also a two-star hotel, El Salam, with 38 rooms at the airport. The real 'pilgrim' accommodation is the guest wing of the monastery itself, which has 200 beds in shared rooms. The charge is at present less than LE 10; those who stay here bring their own food and have the use of kitchens. Only large groups are booked in advance; individuals take their chance, arriving at about 1700, and are checked in by one of the monks, Father George.

There is a special airport about 15 minutes' drive away (Air Sinai runs a twice-weekly service from Cairo, and flights take less than one hour). Or you can drive the 450 kilometres from Cairo.

It is, of course, possible to drive from Suez and there are one or two interesting places en route.

Wells of Moses
The first stopping place is at the Wells of Moses about 30 kilometres, (18 miles) where there is an oasis with a number of wells which legend holds are supplied by water from the rock struck by Moses. Then there is Abu Zneyma where there is a government rest house. The road has followed the coast and there are strange and fascinating coloured fish in the sea here.

Serabit al-Khadam
Ancient turquoise mines exist in the Valley of the Grotto, and inscriptions going back to 3000 BC. At Serabit al-Khadam is the temple with the grotto of Hathor, Our Lady of Sinai, and an inscription of the time of Cheops' father. Here in the Mokattab valley there are writings in a whole range of ancient languages, hieroglyphs, Nabataean, Greek, and Semitic dialects written in characters derived partly from ancient Egyptian and from which the modern European alphabet has evolved.

Coastal resorts
Apart from St Catherine, the chief appeal of Sinai to the visitor is its shores and the maritime treasures of the Gulf of Aqaba and the Red Sea — exquisite coral formations and exotic tropical fish. This is where Egypt's entry into the beach holiday market is finding its principal development. Egypt has a great deal of coastline. As mentioned earlier the Mediterranean shores (and this includes the North Sinai coast) must compete with other Mediterranean resorts. South Sinai, like the Hurghada shores, has more to offer: superb opportunities for diving holidays, and these are attracting many Europeans (especially Germans) and Americans, individually and in groups from diving clubs. New resorts are being developed all the time, with air and road services.

Sharm El Sheikh
At present the best known is Sharm El Sheikh at the extreme southern tip of the peninsula. I flew there from Cairo by Air Sinai (see General Information) and found it a simple but attractive place, lying along a beautiful sandy bay with a small town at the southern end. The town has nothing special to entice the visitor except one good tourist shop — a souk in itself — selling all the usual galebeahs, carvings, leatherwork and so on.

Life here is entirely centred on swimming and diving expeditions. There is one luxury holiday village — Hilton's El Fayrouz — with comfortable air-conditioned chalets and quite good food, graded four-star. Next is the three-star Marina Sharm, a chalet hotel.

Farther along the beach there are two camp sites, Marsa Alaat and Gafy. Sharm has several other less impressive hotels, but one two-star one which appealed to me was the Cliff Top Village which, as the name indicates, is not by the sea but above the town: 30 chalets and an attractive restaurant. For boat services between Sharm and Hurghada see General Information.

Sinai Divers is a German-run diving centre for lessons and guided diving expeditions. They also have a boat with sleeping accommodation which makes tours of several days, diving in different parts of the Gulf of Aqaba. This is particularly popular with Americans.

Dahab

Follow the Gulf of Aqaba coast northwards for 81 kilometres and you come to Dahab. The name means 'gold' and it is said that the Bedouins gave the name to this coast because of the specially gleaming colour of the sands. This is a real oasis, and a 50-chalet Dahab Holiday Village (three-star) has been built; there are camping sites, a diving centre, boats and water ski-ing facilities. There is access by bus from Sharm El Sheikh.

Boy on the Gulf shore

Red Sea Coast and Sinai

Nuweiba and Taba
Another 87 kilometres north lies Nuweiba from which the ferry sails to Aqaba (see General Information). There are two holiday villages here, the four-star El Sayadeen with 66 chalets, and the Nuweiba Holiday Village, three-star with 126 chalets. Palm trees grow — or have been planted — here, which give the place a more 'tropical' look; some of the other new resorts are very bare and arid. For local colour there is a fishermen's village 6 kilometres to the south. Again, there is access by bus from Sharm El Sheikh.

Taba is about another 80 kilometres north, right at the head of the Gulf and on the Egyptian side of the frontier crossing into Israel (Eilat). Jordan's port of Aqaba is on the opposite shore. Here there is the five-star Taba Hilton Hotel and tourist village, and eight kilometres to the south of Taba is a motel called Pharaoh's Island, a pleasant rest-house owned by the Misr Sinai Tourist Company on an island just off the shore, where the ruins of one of Saladin's castles still stand.

Western shore
Down the western side of Sinai — the Gulf of Suez — there is little to attract the visitor. El Tor, about 250 kilometres south of Suez, is the capital of the governorate of South Sinai. It has an airport with a twice weekly flight from Cairo by Air Sinai, but no hotel. Eighty kilometres south again, at the very tip of the peninsula (Sharm El Sheikh is just NE on the Gulf of Aqaba side), is Ras Mohamed. Here are rare and lovely coral reefs and it is the breeding ground for equally rare coloured fishes. But there is no accommodation.

North Sinai

El Arish
Here, on the road route to Tel Aviv, is the governorate's capital El Arish (180 kilometres from the Canal at Qantara East). It has a 16th century ruined castle built by the Turkish Sultan Soliman El-Kanouny on the site of a pharaonic fortress. The town overlooks the Mediterranean and has palm-fringed beaches. There are two five-star hotels, the El Arish Oberoi and the Baron El Arish; Sinai Beach and Sinai Sun Hotels, both graded three-star, and some simpler ones. Air Sinai has regular flights from Cairo to El Arish and there are coach services from Cairo which take seven hours.

Rafah, the second town of North Sinai is also on the Mediterranean shore, on the Egyptian side of the frontier with Israel (the Taba Line) at its northern end. There are some lovely beaches in this area. No regular hotels but some bungalows and tourist camps have been established.

Sinai is now a regular tourist transit region. Not only Israeli visitors but many international tourists come this way after a visit to the Holy Land or Jordan, and Egypt encourages this. For those who stay only in South Sinai for a week there is the no-visa concession (see General Information), but others come through to visit St Catherine and proceed to the Nile, or vice versa.

Most of my travelling in Sinai has been by air, but I was driven from Sharm El Sheikh to St Catherine, a wonderful, spectacular road through brown and red mountains. I was impressed by the excellence of this main road. The journey is roughly 150 kilometres and for the whole way it was a good, wide road, well-surfaced, marked with white lines and international road signs. There are some very dangerous bends and steep hills as you come nearer to St Catherine and they are marked — rightly — with ferocious warnings! Necessary because much of the route is straight, and fast driving. I cannot vouch for the other Sinai main roads, but if this one is a sample they are first-class.

In November 1979 the late President Sadat laid the foundation stone for a religious complex combining the three great monotheist religions of Judaism, Christianity and Islam at St Catherine. That has not yet materialised, but more and more people are finding Sinai a place of peace and welcome. The history of those faiths has shown it a road to safety: for the Jews were led through it to escape the tyranny of the ancient Egyptians, and the infant Jesus was brought in the other direction to escape a Jewish persecution. It is not so many years since these mountain roads were highways of war, but there is a peace in Sinai which is greater than the divisions of mankind.

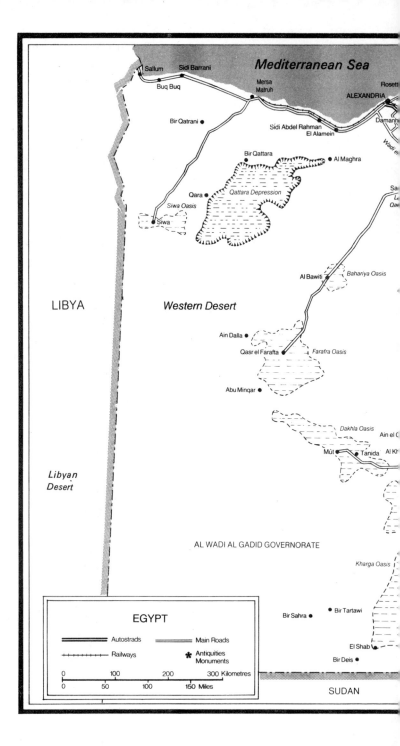

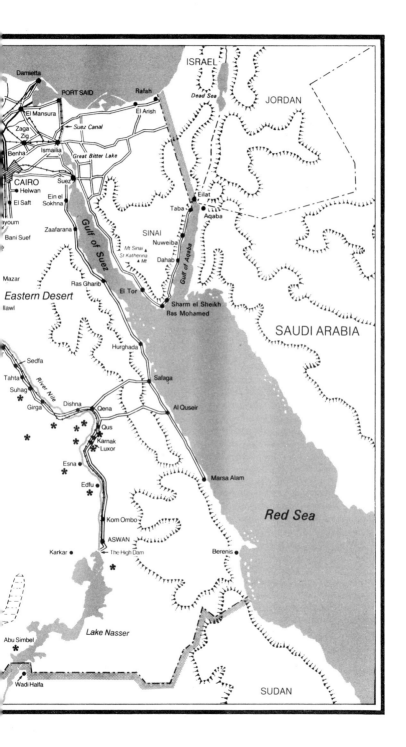

Index